SHAR

SHARING SPACES?

Prayer and the Counselling Relationship

Jessica Rose

DARTON·LONGMAN + TODD

First published in 2002 by
Darton, Longman and Todd Ltd
1 Spencer Court
140-142 Wandsworth High Street
London SW18 4JJ

ISBN 0 232 52387 8

A catalogue record for this book is available from the British Library.

Designed by Sandie Boccacci
Phototypeset in 10/13.25pt Palatino by
Intype London Ltd
Printed and bound in Great Britain by
The Bath Press, Bath

Contents

Acknowledgements

It is impossible to acknowledge all those who have contributed to this book, but there are some in particular who have done so directly, by ideas, by example, and by practical help. Thanks are particularly due to Wendy Robinson (the author of the Foreword), Bishop Basil of Sergievo, Father Michael Fortounatto, Charles Hampton, David Holt, Louise Huish, Michael Seán Paterson and Maggie Tearle. I am also indebted to Bishop Kallistos of Diokleia whose lectures have informed so much of my understanding of the Christian tradition, and to Irina Voiculescu for her support and encouragement. Without my husband, John Rose, it would not have been possible to have had the time or the space to do this work. He has not only provided technical equipment which made the process infinitely easier, but, along with our daughter, Miranda, has put up with the tedious business of living with a writer over many months. Finally, there are those who, as counsellors and clients, have shared so much of their experience. Though they must remain anonymous, it is they who have really written this book.

Foreword

'Do you pray for your clients?' seems a simple question. Nevertheless, when Jessica Rose asked it of her counselling colleagues she found their reactions far from simple. The extent of the expressed interest, anxiety, uncertainty and reticence was far-reaching: the issues involved in bringing together religious faith and professional disciplines appeared to be deep and complex. Working out some of the implications of these discoveries has led to this fascinating and timely book, which is of great value for clients and counsellors alike. It will be useful to both the professional world of counselling (which is not always good at examining its presuppositions, or even its prejudices), and the more church-based schools of care and counselling, encouraging them to be more open to what certain psychological insights can offer.

In *Sharing Spaces?* Jessica Rose moves between different world views – the varied world views of religious belief and the equally varied world views of the counselling profession. Since Thomas Kuhn's breakthrough book, *The Structure of Scientific Revolutions* (Chicago, 1970), there has been more awareness of the power of paradigms (see Chapter 5). Each profession accumulates over time a shared constellation of beliefs, ideas, techniques and ethical values, which demonstrate know-how and disciplined ways of working – a professional paradigm. These paradigms are often held in the form of largely tacit, internalised assumptions. Lives, reputations, empires are built on them. They do not shift easily; too much is at stake. Anomalies in the paradigm, discovered by creative people, push towards new solutions until a paradigm shift is inevitable, and often quite revolutionary in its effects. Each paradigm carries an implicit world view, a cosmology about how the world is and how it works. Inhabitants, or workers, in different paradigms live, in that sense, in different worlds.

Living your life, as some of us do, in and between differing cosmologies is complicated and can be acutely anxiety-provoking. It is noticeable that counsellors interviewed by Jessica Rose were particularly concerned about what their supervisors would make of the fact that they prayed for, or sometimes with, their clients – would it be seen by them as unprofessional conduct, ethically questionable? A counsellor in such a position can end up being seen as too religious by her professional colleagues and too psychological by her religious affiliates – pleasing to neither! To try to do justice to the problems requires a certain juggling skill. From the client's point of view, she may find that her counsellor has a very different tacit world view from her own. What happens when an activity that we call prayer brings cosmologies into collision?

This book offers an examination of some of the differing ways in which people's sufferings, pains and problems are handled by counsellors (with differing and sometimes conflicting theoretical backgrounds) and/or by practitioners of a religious faith (with complex and varied theologies). It sounds like a minefield, and it can be. But the issues involved need to be explored. Jessica Rose manages to do this deftly and with courage. She offers telling vignettes from actual counselling experience, whether as client or counsellor, both from her own work and that of colleagues. She has a good ear for the issues, pitfalls and dilemmas that surround the practice of prayer in this context and illustrates the shifts that can happen in beliefs once illusions are tackled and projections withdrawn. She is excellent on how wary modern 'individuals' are about any hint that some activity like prayer could seem to impinge on their way of understanding their personal liberty. She shows how crippled some clients can feel if they believe they cannot safely bring their religious beliefs into counselling.

This book is concerned to show how the counselling relationship can find its own theological understandings. This involves looking at the central beliefs of the Christian faith – in incarnation, in the Trinity – as underpinning the central emphasis of the counselling profession on the meanings that can only be explored in a deep relationship between counsellor and client. Jessica Rose is brave enough and wise enough to be self-revelatory in some of her stories and illustrations. Insights from her own Orthodox tradition, and certain chosen exemplars from the Greek patristic tradition provide a welcome addition to matters that are more often tackled from a western Catholic or Protestant viewpoint.

This book is a tonic and will open up much lively discussion. It exemplifies the courage it takes to be creative, whether as counsellor or client.

WENDY ROBINSON
Oxford, July 2001

Introduction

We who plague people with words are many nowadays, while those who teach or are taught by actions are very few.[1]

These words predate the invention of the printing press by nearly a thousand years, and the age of information technology by many more. Perhaps less has changed than we think. Yet the author was a prolific writer, and we shall be visiting some of his work during the course of this book.

It is a book which seeks to use words as a vehicle for action. It describes the struggles and the rewards of those who seek to integrate two intensely practical enterprises: prayer and counselling. Each takes us deeper into the inner journey; each affects our relationships with others. If both belong in a person's life and practice, how do they relate to each other? Sometimes it seems the two can go hand in hand; at others they can take us in quite different directions. We shall explore the experiences of those who embark on this dual journey, whether as counsellors or clients, with a view to raising the difficult questions rather than answering them.

Many people have shared in what is presented here, and have given their time to discussing things which affect their everyday lives at a very personal level. Illustrations are also drawn from counselling practice, my own and other people's, though care has been taken to disguise them in such a way that they are not identifiable to any particular person. There are no case histories as such, but there are windows into the way the counselling relationship appears to work. If there is any case history here, it is my own.

The majority of people who find themselves grappling with these two areas have started out from one or the other. A person who prays takes up counselling, or in counselling someone begins to explore the spiritual dimension of life. Somewhere down the road, they begin to ask questions about how or whether the two belong together. In my own case they have always gone side by side. Both began for me, as separate but simultaneous journeys, some fifteen years ago.

Prayer was not new to me. I grew up in a vicarage, steeped in daily prayer and the cycles of the liturgical year but, like many priests' children, I shook the dust of church from off my feet along with that of the family home. It was not that I rejected a particular religious tradition, and continued to believe in God. My father's inability to doubt, it seemed to me, made it impossible for me to believe, and I simply forgot everything to do with it. Only after my father's death did I begin to remember, and it was that which was also the start of my journey in counselling. From the beginning, then, I was aware of two dimensions to what turned out to be a long road towards some kind of healing. For this reason, perhaps, I was always interested in how other people saw the relationship between them. Beginning to ask questions was like taking the lid off a pressure cooker. A huge head of steam had built up inside a great many people: they were desperate to talk.

I also discovered that behind the work that counsellors and their clients do together lies a great wellspring of practical action. Like prayer, it requires us to learn the art of being. At the same time, both the 'talking cure' and prayer rely on, and result in, *doing*. We cannot get very far with either unless we are prepared to make time for them, and allow them to affect the way we live our lives. This is why I describe them as practical disciplines. Most of what is presented here is concerned with the Christian tradition, because I myself have no experience of any other, but it may well have resonances with other faith traditions with which readers are more familiar.

Another discovery was that we cannot embark on counselling without some kind of faith. That may or may not be faith in God, but it is always faith in something: the essential goodness of human beings, perhaps; or the necessity for children to be free from abuse; or a hope that if people can learn to confront what they really feel, the world will be a better place. Counselling lays claim to being free from any particular values, and this should be the case in the sense that it is not for a counsellor to impose anything on a client. There is a mutual exploration, in the course of which both may find that their understanding changes and deepens, but this arises from an attitude of openness to experience. Nevertheless, by the very way they work, and the techniques they adopt, counsellors are committed to a particular way of valuing their fellow human beings. In this book, that commitment is explored in relation to a particular world view, but people arrive at it in many different ways.

This, then, is a practical book. If as a result of reading it people feel freer to ask questions, and relate the work to their own faith, whatever that is, it will have achieved its purpose.

JESSICA ROSE

1
Prayer and counselling: two kinds of relationship

'It is a pity you have to use the word "prayer",' remarked a colleague as she looked through the plans for this book. 'People find it so off-putting. Perhaps if you could talk about meditation, creativity, or even spirituality, it would be so much more accessible.' She was right, and had also hit upon something extremely important: something so important, in fact, that it seemed even more necessary to stay with the word in spite of its difficulties.

Why 'prayer'?
'Prayer' is not a word much in everyday use, even among those who practise it. As a teacher of pastoral care in theological colleges I have often found myself greeted with wry smiles on using the so-called 'P-word'. It is often easier to use some less obvious phrase. 'I will think of you' people say, for example, and they may mean no more or less than that. Thinking of a person can involve bearing someone in mind, meditating on their situation, even a kind of mental 'holding' or companionship which offers love and care even when it is not possible to be physically with them. It may simply mean being affected by someone to the extent that they are constantly thought about in a way that carries no particular significance. Sometimes, however, it means, more or less explicitly, 'I will pray for you.'

If this is the case, if sometimes 'thinking of' is actually a disguise for 'praying for', what difference does this make?

One immediate consequence is that the territory becomes more uncertain. Assumptions come into play, anxieties or hopes may be aroused; it may seem that a particular claim is being made or a promise given. As one counsellor said: 'Prayer is the antithesis of what I am trying to do in my work.' What she meant was that her task is to release clients from other people's expectations, and to find their own path in life, whereas prayer implied having decided what was right for them. She is not alone in finding this an unwelcome intrusion. It was a bishop who remarked, 'I immediately become extremely nervous if I think someone might be praying for something specific for me.'

Yet it is often a need or a crisis of some kind – one's own or someone else's – that turns the mind to prayer. It is well known that people who have not thought about God for years, if at all, will call out for God's help in moments of extreme danger or desperation. Bill Wilson, who was a co-founder of Alcoholics Anonymous,[1] discovered this at the age of thirty-nine, when after years of heavy drinking he found himself in de-tox and close to death. As a young soldier he had had a spiritual experience on visiting Winchester Cathedral which affected him deeply, but in the intervening years alcohol had taken over. Now, near death and in total despair, he called out, 'If there is a God let him show himself!' His cry was followed by an experience of peace and ecstasy such as he had never known. Never again did he doubt the existence of God, and never again did he take another drink. It is perhaps worth noting that to this day AA refrains from attaching any particular dogma or doctrine to the idea of God. In this way many who have been alienated from belief in God by their experiences of religious institutions have been able to develop a relationship with a 'higher power' who can help them to overcome their addiction.

A life-changing experience such as the one Bill Wilson had is comparatively rare, but it illustrates two crucial and related points about prayer as understood by people who pray. Firstly, it involves dialogue in which the other is free to answer or not; secondly, it is rooted in a sense of one's own contingency or incompleteness. This can become apparent through the painful loneliness of a loss or crisis, but it can also be something we discover through joyful or creative experiences. It may arise as we gaze at a beautiful landscape, or at someone we love, or at a work of art, or in the thrill of playing sport with other people, or when we find that something beyond our dreams has occurred. At the heart of a religious attitude – one which turns to God in prayer – is not only need but gratitude, a keen sense of having been given the gift of life, as something one could not have devised for oneself. In the words of Maximos, a seventh-century monk, it is an awareness that 'our very being is on loan to us', and prayer is turning in gratitude to the source of that being.

Someone who eventually became a nun described how this happened to her as a young woman travelling by train across France. She had a sleeping compartment with a small window, and in the night she looked out and saw for the first time the night sky unpolluted by urban light. She was overwhelmed by its beauty and mystery, and this informed her life's journey for decades to come.

An experience like this is not only one of beauty but of awe, as we become aware in a way which can be terrifying of our own smallness and contingency in the vastness of the universe, of how tiny compared with the history of that universe our own human history is. For some people this makes it harder to believe in any kind of God who could be concerned with human beings. We are simply too insignificant in relation to a universe so far ranging in time and space, most of which lies beyond our knowledge or even our imaginations. Others are led by such experiences into an attitude of prayer which takes everything – beauty, success, enjoyment, life itself – as a gift. In this way prayer implies relationship, relationship with whomsoever, whatsoever gives this gift. It belongs, in the language of counselling, to process rather than content. That is, what is actually happening is less relevant than how that happening is experienced. In this way prayer can be as much the province of the scientist as of the priest, of the social worker as of the contemplative.

The word 'prayer', then, takes us into the realm of the personal in a way that the alternatives suggested by my colleague who found the word off-putting do not. Although each one of them would be interesting to explore, they will not help us to look at the very difficult questions which arise when the two enterprises – counselling and prayer – come into contact with each other. Prayer assumes the existence of an 'other', however that other is defined, with whom one has a dialogue. That dialogue often involves other people with whom one is concerned, and there are long-standing traditions of healing through prayer, so that it might seem the two can go quite naturally together.

'Do you pray for your clients?' is, however, a question which any counsellor who prays needs to consider very carefully. It was first put to me by someone who was concerned about the effect prayer might have on the professional nature of counselling. 'After all,' she said, 'if someone thinks they are in a situation with particular boundaries, and the counsellor is also praying for them on the quiet, it is introducing something the client may not expect or want, without them even knowing about it.' To answer this question, or indeed to choose not to answer it, requires us to think carefully about the nature of the relationship between counsellor and client, and what place, if any, the religious discipline of either may have in it.

We are not primarily concerned here with practices often found in specifically Christian counselling circles, where prayer may form an explicit part of the work, but with some of the dilemmas which face people who pray as part of ordinary life, and who are also involved in counselling. For most people who pray, it is seen as something that brings about change and growth. It is an ongoing process, which may not only deepen but also change radically in the course of a person's life. One of the reasons why people are so reluctant to talk about prayer is that it is very personal. Many of us have particular images of what prayer is, but the ways people and communities find of talking to God, however that God may be defined, are many and diverse. What one person regards as prayer might be completely unrecognisable to another, and these differences exist among people whose approaches might well be expected to be similar. I was once present at a conversation between a bishop and a priest, where the latter had raised a great deal of money for a particular project. The bishop asked how this had been done, and the priest replied, 'We prayed, and the money came in.' The bishop said, 'Yes, I see. Your friends chipped in.' It was not a malicious comment. These were both people who spent a great deal of time in prayer, and who respected each other as people of prayer, but their understanding of what was going on was different.

Similarly, if one asks people who pray what they mean by praying for another person, there are, as we shall see, a great many different answers. It is difficult enough for people who pray to find a common language in which to talk about it. For those who do not, it can seem totally opaque, just as it can be extremely difficult to explain to someone who has never experienced counselling what it is that goes on in a session. In both cases there is a process going on, and it is necessary in order to understand it to enter into it, or at least to have some experience with which to compare it. The extent to which these things can be discussed at the level of concepts or ideas is extremely limited. Both disciplines have consequences for those who take part in them, and the experience of those who practise both can provide insights into areas where they are incompatible as well as where they may work together.

It will be clear to anyone who has read this far that what is being described here is a subjective response, which is not objectively measurable or even easily describable. One of the difficulties in exploring the questions that are raised in this book is that, whether one is talking about prayer or about counselling, it is not possible to be precise in any objective sense about what is going on. In both cases, something appears to happen which the participants regard as significant, but the how or the why cannot be definitively stated. We do know that, in both disciplines, certain practices are helpful. We also know that both are subject to the unexpected and the inexplicable.

Why counselling?

As far as counselling is concerned, there are libraries full of research on what it is, if anything, that is achieved, and how. Researchers come up against all sorts of difficulties as soon as they try to quantify the results of counselling. Presumably it should ultimately make us feel better than we did, but how do we measure that? We can score people on indices of emotional well-being, for example, and compare where they come before and after a series of sessions. Apart from being a subjective variable, however (one for which there is no standard scientific measurement, as there is, say, for height or weight), a sense of emotional well-being may not necessarily correlate with the healing of emotional pain. Not only do things tend to get worse before they get better, but in the process of getting in touch with our emotions we may become sensitised to pain in new ways. Sometimes counselling comes to an end when a person has reached the point where they are ready to make certain changes in their life. The level of dissatisfaction may actually be higher than when they started.

Even if we try to assess something more measurable such as the ability to function at work or in relationships, counselling occurs in the context of an ongoing life, in which we do not know what other factors may be involved. As in physical injury or illness, time itself may make more difference than anything else to the healing of emotional wounds.

Assuming, however, that counselling is an effective process, researchers generally agree that the most significant healing factor does not lie in particular techniques or theories, but in the quality of relationship between counsellor and client.[2] Any relationship between human beings carries potential for healing, but at the same time the possibility of damage; and to enter into any relationship involves taking a risk. For this reason the counselling world rightly pays close attention to the dangers – on both sides – of intimate involvement with another person: dangers of power being abused, of unresolved dependency, of exploitation and so on. It is committed to providing a safe and accepting environment in which clients can explore their story, their life situation and their responses without being judged or told what to do, the hope being that this will enable them to find a way through which is authentic for them.

Whatever the theoretical background of the counsellor, there are three core elements which help to establish the relationship and make it effective. One is the ability to get inside another person's frame of reference and understand how he or she is feeling, while at the same time holding back and not imposing one's own views. This is the capacity for empathy, which together with a certain reticence can help people to find their own solutions. There is also a necessity to be able to overcome one's own embarrassment or timidity sufficiently to be able to address openly what is going on in the relationship itself, the positives and the negatives. Add to these a highly developed self-awareness on the part of the counsellor, and we have a cocktail of relationship skills that are extremely powerful. In themselves they are not good or bad, only potent. They are equally of use to the advertising executive or even the torturer as to the counsellor.

Because of this the counselling establishment is rightly concerned to safeguard its clients from abuse, especially given the very personal and confidential nature of counselling. However much there is in the way of training, accreditation and supervision of counsellors, the primary factor at work is a relationship between two people, largely conducted in private, where neither party meets people associated with the other, and whose outcome cannot ultimately be monitored or objectively measured.

An important aspect of these safeguards is keeping to

particular boundaries of time and space. They impose a certain discipline which helps to focus the work, and remind both parties of the task in hand. Sooner or later this often means that the client will begin to question the authenticity of the relationship. 'How can this be genuine when you will only see me at 4 o'clock on a Thursday?' or 'when I pay you for your time?', or 'when I am only here for you to help me and know nothing about you and your problems?' 'What happens if I am in real distress at the weekend?' These are questions which counsellors and clients have to grapple with in order to reach an understanding of what they are trying to achieve, and how the particular relationship they have can contribute to it.

The boundaries themselves are open to abuse. Instead of leading to a deeper experience, they can be used simply as a defence. The counsellor can withdraw into professionalism, and the client can deny that there is any real engagement because of the conditions that surround the work. At best, however, like the seal of the confessional, they provide a *temenos*, a place set apart, in which it is possible to express what cannot otherwise be expressed, and to allow otherwise unsafe feelings to emerge and begin to be managed.

It is this quality of relationship – flawed though it may often be – which is at the heart of the counselling process, and which is explored in this book in relation to prayer. The question being asked is, 'What happens when two people are working together in counselling, which is a contracted, professional relationship, and one or both of them is also engaged in prayer?'

In the understanding of many people who pray, prayer is concerned with breaking down the barriers between people. Boundaries of time and space become *less* important. Relationships with God and with other human beings may come to be understood in new ways which transcend presence and absence, and even death itself. In praying for others, many people experience themselves as offering a channel or window through which God can act. 'How,' they might say, 'since God is love, could this possibly be damaging?' Yet, it could also be said that since any effort at prayer will fall short of perfection, placing oneself in this position risks introducing one's own material between God and the other: material which could be damaging, particularly if we have a strong investment in the outcome.

Prayer and counselling: allies or strangers?
There are many anxieties which can arise when these two worlds overlap, and these are explored in this book through the experience of those involved, both counsellors and clients. On the one hand, if prayer is an important part of one's life, should it be left out of an exploration leading to greater self-understanding? On the other hand, assumptions and beliefs are involved in both, and these may diverge in important ways.

It is not unusual, for example, for a client who engages regularly in prayer to be uncomfortable about asking for psychological help. 'Shouldn't prayer be enough?' is a question that is often asked. 'Isn't this self-indulgent?' A specific problem may arise when someone has received the prayer of others for healing and nothing seems to have changed. It can happen that the person prayed for is blamed for this by those who did the praying. 'You have not received the grace that was offered,' they may be told, or 'You are resisting God's help.' For such a person seeking out a counsellor as a non-judgemental helper, the idea of being prayed for by that counsellor could be terrifying, and make working together impossible.

Again, where a religious upbringing has been particularly strict or even abusive, this may make the idea of prayer frightening or even repellent. A counsellor who was used to praying with her clients realised this would be counter-productive with someone who came to see her who had been brought up with the idea that she was a sinful, horrible child. 'I had to be very careful with her,' she said, 'and I didn't pray aloud with her at all until we had been through the whole business of the abuse and what it did, and she could see she was not condemned.'

Counsellors vary in the extent to which praying for clients troubles them. For some it comes as naturally as breathing to integrate their religious life with their practice, while for others there is a constant struggle to reconcile the two disciplines. Take, for example, someone who begins training as a counsellor and who has already an established and regular practice of personal and/or communal prayer. It may even be this which has prompted him or her to want to help others more effectively. Hopefully, training will provide new skills in deepening relationships and developing empathy, and the counsellor will begin to work with these skills with people in various kinds of distress. This can place a great strain on personal resources, particularly at the beginning, and, as in any time of crisis, prayer may become particularly important. It may also happen, however, that with all the changes that are going on, the well-known and trusted ways of praying lose their previous significance, particularly as the person comes into contact with new depths of suffering and trauma through the work.

A young man in this situation went into a church to pray, feeling very disturbed within himself. It was a Catholic church, and the bread and wine from the Mass were preserved in a tabernacle, in a side chapel where a lamp was lit. He settled himself there and tried to pray, but found it extremely difficult to know where to begin. As he was sitting there a man burst in, marched up to the tabernacle and shook his fist at it. 'I've had enough!' he shouted. 'I won't tolerate this behaviour any longer!' He hit the tabernacle with his fist, and walked out again. 'Now that,' thought the young man sitting quietly in the chapel, 'that was prayer!'

Counselling training, properly done, expands our consciousness, and this in itself is likely to lead to questioning of oneself and one's beliefs, so that many people who go into such training with a religious faith find they go through great uncertainty about what it is they do believe. Previous experiences of talking with God in prayer may begin to look doubtful or untrustworthy set against new understandings of one's own psychological history. Even if there is no such crisis of faith, new counsellors may begin to wonder whether they are keeping to professional boundaries if they take problems involving clients into their prayer. Are they being sufficiently detached? Do they have any right to pray about what has been brought to them as a professional?

A minister who was on his first placement as a trainee counsellor became very concerned about a young woman client – a lapsed Roman Catholic – who was suicidal. It seemed to him that she was cut off from the love of God, which he himself found so sustaining, and he longed to be able to help her rediscover her faith. This, after all, would be his job in his role as minister. As a counsellor, however, he felt he had no right to use this kind of language in their sessions, and this was very painful for him. He did, however, pray for her in private, and as a result he decided to refer her to a more experienced counsellor.

Many counsellors would see the very idea of introducing prayer in any form into the professional relationship as wrong. Even if the client is prayed for in private, there is a possibility that such prayer could be a form of unconscious influence on the other, and this is something that must be taken seriously. Counsellors usually become important to their clients during the course of their work together, and it is all too easy to influence others without overtly suggesting anything. We have only to look at ways in which children live out the hopes and disappointments of their parents without ever having been consciously aware of them. A missionary of some thirty years' experience described how, when he entered into this work as a young man, he subsequently discovered that his parents had been praying that he should do this since before he was born. In his own case, he was, nevertheless, satisfied that it had been the right choice.

Clients entering into counselling often ask what a counsellor's religious stance is, and counsellors differ in their response to this. Some are prepared to disclose it, while others are not, but most are agreed it is important to try to discover why this question is important for the client. For religious clients it may be important to know that their beliefs and practice are not going to be seen as an escape from reality, or explained away in psychological terms. Sometimes, well into the counselling work, clients will say something about their religious practice as though testing how it will be received: 'I prayed about it' or 'I went into the church and lit a candle'. Often these statements will either be hedged about with disclaimers such as 'It may sound daft but . . .', or slipped into the conversation in such a way that they could easily be overlooked. At the same time, there are others who seek reassurance that the counsellor is not religious, since to the client this implies he or she is more likely to judge, or preach. People seeking counselling are often in need of refuge from an environment – religious or otherwise – where everyone else seems to have all the answers.

Nevertheless there are points of contact between the two disciplines. Both are concerned with nourishing the human person, and becoming more true to who one is. Both share the accusation of seeming strange and cultic, or a means of avoiding the real world. The life of a counsellor is often paradoxically lonely, many hours a week being spent in intimate contact with people, yet bound by confidentiality so that he or she is carrying a great deal of other people's story and feelings without being able to share these, except in supervision. In contemporary society, a life of prayer can also be something of a desert experience, poorly understood in society at large, and insufficiently nourished in the churches. It was startling to be approached by a client who knew I was a member of a Christian church, who said that she did not want my help with her depression, because she understood it well enough. What she wanted was to explore its spiritual significance. 'And,' she said, 'the vicar doesn't talk about those things.' Whatever one's beliefs, sharing honestly about personal matters is difficult and easily avoided, and this is as true of the spiritual life as it is of the traditional preserves of counselling.

At the same time there are ways in which prayer and counselling sit uncomfortably together. While both may be involved in healing, counselling has no religious dogma attached to it, and religious beliefs do not naturally lie within its areas of discussion. Its immediate focus, whatever its wider effects in society, is the individual. The religious life, on the other hand, places a high value on membership of a community, even though this may be seen in very different ways in different traditions. Healing is seen less as a matter of personal fulfilment than as a question of finding a right relationship with the transcendent and with humanity at large. A choice which might seem sacrificial and the right path to take from a religious perspective, can appear pathological in a counselling context.

In a discussion on how counsellors integrate prayer and professional practice, someone asked why it had taken so long for someone to ask such an obvious question. Perhaps it has something to do with the fact that it highlights areas that require deeply personal answers. They touch on practice at the level of what we believe about the very nature of human beings and our relationships with each other. In what follows, many have shared generously and often painfully, but also sometimes with a great sense of relief, in order to help in these explorations.

2

Talking with people who pray

Where, when and how do counsellors and their clients pray? There are many different ways of entering into prayer, which may be spontaneous or planned, alone or with others, with or without words. The various ways described here have one thing in common: prayer is experienced as a conversation. A person praying is prepared to listen as well as to speak; it is a dialogue with the divine, however the divine may be understood by the person who prays. This does not mean that the other side of that dialogue is always obvious. Indeed, there may be long periods when nothing appears to happen at all, but part of the process of prayer is listening, in the broadest sense. What is received may not necessarily be something that can be put into words. In prayer a person may experience her or himself as held or comforted, challenged or changed in some way. It may be that the 'answer' is experienced as coming at some other time altogether, but is linked with prayer in the mind of the person concerned.

While prayer can involve doing particular things at particular times, people who pray do not always define its boundaries very precisely. A Jewish counsellor, for example, was reluctant to describe herself as praying for her clients because it suggested she might be allowing something to intrude on the therapeutic process. Nevertheless, she said, 'I do think about them prayerfully.' By this she meant that she would often have them in mind during services at the synagogue. On further reflection she added that thinking about them at these times could be called prayer when she felt something shift within herself.

Many people set aside time to pray: at home, in church, walking the dog and so on. A surprising amount of prayer goes on while people are driving, since for many this is the only time they are alone. Prayer can be part of beginning the working day, or something that goes on during it. Some people finish work with prayer, committing all that has happened into the hands of God, and marking the transition to ordinary life. Some counsellors who pray focus specifically on their work. Others, though they might be people who pray, do not find it necessary or appropriate to do so. Yet others are unsure, like the counsellor quoted above, as to whether they would describe what they do as prayer. Similarly, prayer may be part of the inner work of people engaged in counselling as clients, especially between sessions. Where this is so, the effect on the client and images evoked may form part of the content of counselling. In some circumstances, where there is explicitly a shared faith, counsellors and clients might pray together, especially at the beginning or end of a session.

There are parallels between the disciplines involved in prayer and in counselling. A regular practice of prayer involves taking time to set aside the distractions of everyday life, and this is also true of the counselling session, and sometimes of inner work between sessions. Whether or not they have a religious faith, counsellors and clients often take time before or at the beginning of a session to centre themselves in order to concentrate on the work in hand. One counsellor described her working day as entering into a 'psychic soup', where her quality of attention was different from ordinary interactions, and where she felt more vulnerable than usual. Within this 'soup' she was making herself available at a different and deeper level. For religious people, the centring process may include reminding themselves of God's presence, committing the work to God, or asking for a blessing on it. 'My prayer before sessions is for clarity of mind,' said one counsellor, 'for help to be the best counsellor I can be in this situation, not for any supernatural revelation.' In either case, there is a reorientation, and a conscious attempt to listen and participate at a deeper level than the everyday.

Ritual also plays an important part in both disciplines. In counselling, time boundaries, ways of greeting and saying goodbye, the attitude to touch, the arrangement of the room and its furniture are all usually consistent and meaningful. An exploratory session with the daughter of a therapist took place largely in an uncomfortable silence. After half an hour she pointed angrily to a bowl of stones and fir cones and spoke for the first time: 'My mother's got a bowl of crap like that.' As the daughter of a priest I was reminded of my own anger during a time when entering a church would take me unwillingly and uncomfortably into a familiar world which I had rejected.

Maintaining attention

Entering a particular physical and psychic space does not, of course, necessarily involve prayer, but it does assist us in paying attention to ourselves and each other in a way which affects both parties, and may give rise to unexpected experiences. Someone whose counsellor began sessions by waiting in silence described it as comparable to a time when he had become angry with a God he did not believe in and had cried out to him in desperation to tell him what to do. From somewhere, inside or outside himself he could not tell, came the words: 'You are created to find your own meaning.' The silence of the counsellor produced a similar sense of the vast emptiness into which he had shouted, and he experienced her as absent, although she felt that she was paying close attention.

The quality of attention required of a counsellor involves being able to observe what is occurring inside oneself as well as in the room, while remaining alert to the theoretical implications of what is going on. Maintaining this kind of vigilance is hard work, and when counsellors pray, it is often in order to manage this better than they would be able to do alone. Tackling intimate material, including the stuff of the relationship itself, may make it very difficult to remain attentive while keeping at bay three major enemies of good practice: retaliation against attack, denial of the seriousness of the problem, and identification with the other person. At such times anyone might feel under pressure and begin to question their own competence. A counsellor described it as working so hard to keep control that she couldn't 'use what feels to me like the creative source . . . the bit that flows like a river underneath'.

Finding themselves in this situation some counsellors inwardly use 'arrow prayers', short requests fired as from a bow, such as 'Help me', and these are sometimes followed by an experience of being answered. A couple counsellor described this as bringing something into the atmosphere, or putting herself in a place where something could come through. In terms of her beliefs, it was a way of helping herself hear what the Holy Spirit had to say. On one such occasion she found herself extremely anxious because the wife of a couple was in a very dark mood, which tended to intensify during the sessions. Within herself she prayed a brief prayer for help, and at that moment became less concerned with her own reactions and more aware of the fragility of the person in front of her. As a result she was able to help the woman to name her depression, and seek medical help.

Another counsellor described how he will sometimes pray when he is panicking during a session and does not know what to do. 'I am thinking, "God help me to get focused here. Help me to contain this panic." ' At other times when he was particularly relaxed, he would become aware of things flowing well, 'and I might sort of say to God, almost like a check, "Is what is going on here helpful?" It's not that I'm clutching at straws, but I am also praying.'

When wound touches wound

In psychological terms, what is needed to relate openly with others is a relatively fluid internal world, one which can allow itself a degree of disintegration without becoming threatened or needing to foreclose. Although a breadth of experience helps us to understand others, what is unhealed in us may cause over-identification with the other, and this can get in the way of being able to help. For instance, a young doctor found himself increasingly unable to pay attention to patients and their relatives in the Accident and Emergency Department in which he worked. Being a conscientious and compassionate person this disturbed him and he sought counselling. It emerged that he had been devastated by the death of a close friend (also in his twenties) from cancer, not only because of the death itself, but also because the medical treatment his friend had received was invasive and painful. It was very difficult for him to come to terms with how this affected his identity as a doctor as well as the grief and the fear of mortality engendered by the death. Through counselling he was able to stop blaming himself and begin to address these difficulties.

As counsellors, in particular, if our own wounds are too raw or too firmly covered up for fear of pain, it may not be possible to accompany others on the journey that they need to make. In supervision a counsellor described how difficult it was for her to sit through sessions with two particular people, both of whom were threatened by terminal illness. They had both begun to work with her at around the same time, as sometimes happens: more than one person presents with a problem which is especially difficult for the counsellor, almost as though there is something she or he especially needs to hear. In this particular instance it emerged that there had been a family crisis a year or two previously when a close relative had been diagnosed as having cancer. As is often the case, the counsellor had spent a lot of time supporting other family members and had not had any opportunity to talk through what it had meant to her. Identifying this enabled her to get in touch with her own feelings, and so become freer to work with the people in question.

On a professional level this is familiar enough. Prayer was also involved here, since after supervision that was where the counsellor took her questions about death. Prayer helped her confront her own fears, and this was important in becoming able to help these clients face what death meant to them. Particularly, perhaps, when we have firm convictions, it is important to test them against our own experience, and this was what the situation compelled her to do. For someone who prays this may involve questioning God, and learning to protest in prayer, as part of coming to terms with what God will not 'put right', at least in human terms. In this instance, owning her own fear and frustration meant that she was less tempted to bypass the emotions of her clients. She had begun to face how difficult it was to contemplate death even within the framework of her own Christian beliefs.

Within a particular faith tradition, prayer might take the form of using stories from that tradition to come to terms with one's own limitations. One counsellor was helped by the story of the Good Samaritan (Luke 10:30-7), where a man is attacked and left wounded by the roadside. A Levite (one of the priestly caste) crosses over and ignores him, and it is a Samaritan (a marginalised foreigner) who stops to help. The counsellor was struck by a meditation she heard read in church in which the Levite was described as having ignored the man because he was unable to bear the sight of his wounds: 'When the Levite saw me, injured and in pain, thinking my wounds incurable and unable to endure the sight of them, he passed by on the other side.'[1] Counsellors, like anyone else, can find themselves in the position of the Levite as described here, not because they do not care but because the caring is more than they can bear. The meditation became a resource whereby she was able to accept her own difficulty in coming close to the pain of her clients, and begin to find ways to address it.

Containing difficult feelings

There are also times when it becomes hard for a counsellor to maintain a compassionate stance because he or she feels attacked or annoyed or bored within the relationship. This is not only uncomfortable; it generates guilt and anxiety: 'Surely I shouldn't be feeling like this?' Yet failure to acknowledge such problems will only get in the way of a solution. This is well known to those who work directly with the relationship through the transference. 'Transference' is a technical term for a phenomenon used by some counsellors to understand the client's emotional history. In the relatively uncluttered relationship with the counsellor, about whom the client knows very little, feelings which have previously been attached to significant others, such as parents, become 'transferred' to the counsellor. By observing and interpreting the transference, the counsellor can help the client gain insight into these feelings, and it can also then be possible to test their relevance in the current situation, as a means of uncovering emotional patterns in which the client is stuck.

Nevertheless, such feelings are sometimes acted out, especially if they are not worked through. An inexperienced counsellor was at her wits' end because of a client who was given to ringing her at home during the night, in a great state of distress. She did not know how to address the situation or stop it happening. Coming home from a party in the small hours of a Sunday morning, she found herself phoning the client. When the call was answered she said, 'I just thought I would see how you are.' Particularly where a contract is less than clear, or the motivation of the client uncertain, a counsellor can come to feel not only thoroughly deskilled, but also put upon and angry. She or he is making all the running, sticking faithfully to arrangements, only to find the other person has not turned up, finds reasons to come late or leave early, or calls on other people for help. This behaviour usually signals a depth of pain and fear and, though distressing, is a valuable clue to the plight of the client, and an opportunity to react in a way which may change something. It is important, of course, to identify the issues in supervision, but prayer may also be a place where it is possible to acknowledge the resentment and transcend it.

Prayer is not a substitute for supervision, but some of those who pray experience it as providing similar support in difficult situations. A Christian counsellor, for example, described

himself as having an 'internal divine supervisor', not so much
an external God as someone who could be met or experienced
within, and who tuned in to the space between himself and
his client. The sense of this presence was stabilising, enabling
him to keep a professional stance at the same time as being
open to the person he was with. 'God served the function of
supervisor for me, being able to help me contain the awfulness
of what I was feeling.' Another said, 'I think [what happens
in prayer] is similar to what happens to feelings when you
express them to a supervisor. It is a relationship which acts as
a container, and I receive some understanding so that I am
not just thinking, "I hate this person," but actually remember
that I used to love them as well. It helps me to get a clearer
picture.'

Again, a Jewish counsellor described how she deals with
difficult moments in the session. She allows herself to relax in
order to contact a deeper level of wisdom: 'Hopefully,' she
added, 'she answers.' Such an experience does not, of course,
necessarily imply religious belief. The phenomenon of the
internalised supervisor is well documented (e.g. by Patrick
Casement[2]). Yet in calling this prayer, the people concerned
are suggesting something more than a psychological process
whereby we internalise the support we receive from another.
They are positing the existence of a transcendent being who
has an independent existence; contact may be experienced
within, but it is with someone who lies beyond our own
internal world.

Unexpected change
Particularly in the early stages of practice, counsellors spend
time between sessions thinking about the people they work
with, and many clients also do a great deal of work on their
own between sessions. For some this includes prayer: an
attempt to bring the work into the presence of God. In the
process people sometimes discover themselves changed.

This was the experience of a counsellor in a hospital chap-
laincy who prayed regularly for her clients between sessions.

'I try to see each one as God would see them.' This helped
her to understand each one of the people she worked with as
a unique human being. It also enabled her to stand back from
trying to solve their problems: she could accept that there was
far more between them and God than she knew or would
ever know. Prayer became very important to her when she
was working with a dying man who was a convinced atheist,
and whose wife had made it very clear that she too was an
atheist and did not want any religious input. The counsellor
found this difficult, because as an evangelical Christian she
believed that it was necessary to confess belief in God before
death in order to be saved. She had great respect for both the
man and his wife, and though religious matters were never
discussed with either of them, she prayed for them in private.

When the time came that the man was close to death, the
counsellor was summoned, along with the Roman Catholic
chaplain who had also been helping them, and she arrived
just after he had died. He was surrounded by his family, and
she was struck by the atmosphere of love in the room, as
something almost tangible. One of the children asked her if
she thought her father would have gone to hell because he
did not believe in God. 'Would you send your father to hell?'
she replied. 'No,' said the child, and the counsellor said that
she did not think God would do so either. Later she was
surprised to find that the Roman Catholic chaplain had given
the same response to the same question, and even more so
that the experience had profoundly changed her own beliefs.

Again, a counsellor who was brought up as a Roman Catholic but has little involvement with any institutional Church ('a
pre-establishment Christian' as she described herself), usually
visits a church building on her way home from work. Here
she often lights candles as a symbol of her prayers for her
clients continuing even as she returns to home and family. On
one such occasion she found herself praying out of a sense
of despair about a young man, a drug addict, who seemed
fundamentally impossible to help. Whatever was offered in
the way of support seemed to act as a poison to his system.

The counsellor and other professionals had done everything they could to get him into rehabilitation but it always broke down. Shortly after the episode in the church when she had become quite desperate, the man agreed for the first time to enter a residential programme, and stayed. To the counsellor, this was the action of something beyond any human agency.

Stories of this kind question the non-directive nature of counselling practice. It can be very hard to accept that there may be no recognisable result, not to want something to come right for the client. The counsellor's involvement with this young man meant that his plight touched her deeply at a point where, having taken her professional expertise as far as it could go, she found herself asking for help from her God, whom she also believed to love him. Her prayer was not for a particular outcome, but was: 'No one can help this boy. You help him', – a point of desperation which is commonly reached by counsellors at the very brink of breakthrough, when the tension can be such that one is tempted to abandon the work altogether. Praying can be a way of easing that tension and staying with the situation. Certainly for the counsellor it was a highly significant event, which she described as 'evidence of things unseen'. It was not that her work had been useless, but more as though the very intensity of her involvement had created a union of energies between the human level of action and the divine love which she believed to lie beyond it. The power of each was enhanced by the other.

Praying together and talking about prayer
Overt, shared prayer within a session sometimes takes place in counselling organisations with a religious basis, or where a client has chosen a particular counsellor because of a shared faith. Some find this helpful because it places the work within a context that is in harmony with their spiritual path. Clients may also wish to discuss prayer, though they may not always feel they have licence to talk about it. Someone came to see me for counselling once a week for two years before she plucked up courage to ask if I had read any of the books on

prayer which were on my bookshelf. It often seems that opposite taboos operate in the therapeutic and the religious worlds. It is acceptable to talk to one's therapist about sex and to one's priest about prayer but not vice versa. Both are probably equally difficult to talk about sincerely and personally. There may also be a fear of religious behaviour being treated as superstitious or pathological, or interpreted as avoidance.

What a person says about how they pray and for whom can be very revealing. A woman who had been sexually abused as a child described going into church and praying for various people she loved. The counsellor asked her if she had also prayed for herself since she was living through some very distressing circumstances at the time. 'No,' replied the client. 'Why not?' 'Because I don't think God could possibly be interested in me.'

Some counselling, however, uses prayer directly as a tool with which to heal a person's psychological wounds, or free them from an abusive relationship, or from some occult influence. The counsellor would seek to discern which of these was primarily at work and pray accordingly. 'I often talk with a client about how we shall pray,' said one such counsellor, 'and try to put the responsibility on the client. I am trying to encourage the client's own relationship with God.' She described this kind of prayer as 'sitting side by side before God', knowing that it is God who is the healer. In such situations a session may end by summing up what has been talked about and asking for forgiveness, healing, release or protection as seems appropriate.

For example, someone who was having severe panic attacks was referred by her GP for short-term counselling within the medical practice. This helped her, as she learned strategies for controlling the feelings of panic when they occurred. Later on, she decided to explore the origins of her panic, and started seeing a Christian counsellor who also worked with prayer. Together they worked on anger and fear which she had never been able to express before, and at the end of each session they prayed for her release from fear. One day she said that she had had a panic attack on going into a large crowded hall, and her mother said, 'Your grandmother was like that.' There was no access to any particular story in the family which might account for this, so the counsellor suggested that they could pray for her release from whatever negative influence might be being passed down the generations, even though they might never know its origins. The client found this very helpful, not just because she believed in prayer, but also because it highlighted for her how difficult it was to be herself. 'If I can be free,' she said, 'I can be myself and not like my mother or my grandmother.'

A dual journey

This particular counsellor, although she saw prayer as the instrument of healing, was very concerned to set it in the context of her clients' feelings. All too often, in a religious context, dogma is poured on raw wounds only making them more painful. People are exhorted to forgive too quickly, or pass over their grief, and the process of confronting feelings through counselling is seen as self-indulgent. Nevertheless, psychological and spiritual healing can go side by side. For example, a woman who in counselling was working through very painful memories of sexual abuse, found that the feelings tended to surface while she prayed. They were unmanageable when she was alone so she would try to push them away. At these times she felt that God said to her, 'Wait until you see [the counsellor] and bring them up then, when there are two of you together.'

Again, people who belong to a church or other religious community may go to counselling to get in touch with the problem and then ask a minister or priest to pray with them for healing. This might involve spontaneous prayer, or a particular ritual. There might, for example, be a communion service during which a copy of the family tree is placed on the altar, or a memorial service in which family members are named and prayed for. For some people the rite of confession or reconciliation may be part of this process, seen as a way of healing the separation from God which has been brought about by emotional damage.

It can also be through prayer of this kind that people decide to go into counselling. 'I have been to confession,' said a young man who had been arrested for soliciting in public toilets, 'but although I have received absolution I don't feel I have really understood yet what I did. I don't feel right with God.' In counselling, he was able to look at ways in which the soliciting was a form of sexual addiction by which he smothered the pain of having been himself abused as a child. Eventually he was able to move on from this compulsion, rather than getting caught up in a cycle of doing, confessing, and then feeling compelled to do it again. At the same time, his religious faith, and his desire not to behave in this way because of what he believed, was an important part of the process. The counselling was a means not only to stopping the behaviour, but also to being able to receive the forgiveness offered by the priest.

Being in counselling can itself affect prayer. Often people find that as their inner world expands psychologically their ways of praying change. A woman who was working through a family crisis which challenged her lifelong faith and perception of God's care, prayed over a long period in two quite different ways. There seemed to be a 'day-time' God who was found in church and who had all the attributes of patriarch, creator, judge, manager; and a 'night-time God' met in the privacy of her insomnia, who was compassionate and with her in the painful searchings of her heart. As someone who had been strictly brought up in a particular tradition she was fearful of naming the latter process as prayer. Such changes can be confusing. At the same time, inner work which would otherwise have to be done within the counselling session may take place in prayer, as a person wrestles with the wounds which are emerging into consciousness.

A sense of belonging

Another aspect of prayer which counsellors and clients can find helpful is that it is not an isolated experience. It is part of the tradition of prayer that it takes place in the context of a community, which may be defined in many different ways. A Roman Catholic client, for example, would refer to the 'communion of saints' as something that sustained him during a period when the work was deep and the gap between weekly sessions seemed long. In terms of his beliefs this meant that although he was struggling with very difficult material, he was part of a community of prayer which included the whole Church, all those who also suffered and prayed and trusted in God. Just as a story or legend may help a person to feel less isolated, he was also able to draw on stories that he knew of people, living and dead, who were part of this network of prayer.

Psychologically a belief of this kind can be very important. The psychoanalyst Donald Winnicott said that our psychological health depends on our membership of something – even the local bowls club will do[3] – and an experience of prayer which gives a sense of belonging to and connection with the whole of the human race throughout our history is likely to be sustaining. This is also reflected in the religious practice of some counsellors who make a point of praying for their clients at religious services, in the belief that this draws them into the prayer of the community. One such counsellor, a Christian, who usually goes to a communion service midweek, carries a list of names with her to the communion rail: 'It's almost like bringing them with me to the table, asking God to feed them and bless them.'

The counsellor who referred to entering a 'psychic soup' was touching on something comparable: her sense of being part of something shared by human beings generally. This dimension can be extremely important in the counselling process through, for example, music, art or literature. A woman who was struggling with extreme separation anxiety, so that she found it very difficult to live through the space between weekly sessions, found a piece of music – the slow movement of a Shostakovich piano concerto – which helped her to feel safe. 'I could fall off a cliff into it,' she said, an apt comment since her anxiety between sessions made her feel she was falling into oblivion. Listening to the music helped her to manage the gaps between sessions, and gradually become more confident of her own survival. It also helped her to place herself in a wider context than the very intense relationship she had with her counsellor, since her love for this piece of music not only gave her a sense of relationship with the composer, but with the many others who had performed or listened to it over the years. One of the most intractable situations is when work is progressing well within the one-to-one relationship, but the person involved has no sense of belonging to anything – family, sports team, workplace or whatever it may be – in the outside world. It is very hard to nourish the spirit in those circumstances.

It can, of course, be argued that to introduce religious or other resources in this way is a form of avoidance, diluting the counselling process. Often healing involves working through an experience of intimacy and deep dependency which is extremely painful. Such experiences can be understood in terms of regressing to emotional states from early childhood, and for counsellors who work with the transference in particular, it is important to be able to tolerate and confront these in order to help the client develop a strength of ego which was prevented earlier by trauma of one kind or another. It could therefore be a mistake to draw too quickly on religious resources even when they are available, and it is essential that they are not used to *bypass* the complexities of the counselling relationship. An understanding of human relationships which transcends one-to-one intimacy cannot be imposed, but it may emerge from experience.

An example of this occurred when my mother died. For the previous two years her illness had meant I was constantly having to respond to crises at some distance from where I lived and worked. Though difficult to manage, this did not cause any unplanned disruption to the work, but when she eventually died, I found I needed time to recover before I was ready to work again and I took four weeks off. This was a long break without warning to people for whom breaks were difficult even when carefully planned. I decided to explain the reason for my absence since it seemed unnecessarily harsh to disappear for a month without doing so, but it raised questions. Would my grief be perceived as excessive, that I put my own needs before those of people whom I had encouraged to trust me to be reliably there for them? Or would it perhaps seem insufficient, if I was back at work in a mere four weeks? How would it affect those who had themselves been bereaved and whose bereavement formed part of our work? Would they in particular feel able to continue to talk about those things knowing I had experienced a bereavement myself? All these questions and many more arose in the weeks, indeed months, following my return to work, and there was inevitably a range of reactions to be worked with.

During my absence, however, several people from the practice wrote or sent cards, and one or two kept in touch by letter throughout the period. Whatever the transferences that had to be worked with subsequently, these pieces of correspondence were extraordinarily precious and nourishing, not only as gestures of genuine concern, but also as affirming the mutuality of the counselling relationship. One letter in particular, from someone who herself was working through a major bereavement, and who found holiday breaks very difficult, described how she had discovered through my loss that she was not alone: not only I but many other people were sharing in the same experience. She herself negotiated with exquisite sensitivity a closeness which held me in mind, and a separateness which took great care not to intrude, and she explicitly took upon herself to manage the difficulty my absence caused her while I was away. She would not have used the language of prayer or religious belief, but her handling of the situation was an act of faith in our relationship.

Nevertheless, while faith of any kind can be a resource in psychological healing, it can also be used as a powerful defence. God can be set up as fixer, judge, scapegoat or alternative companion in ways that create barriers to self-discovery, relationship and personal responsibility. A young woman reached a state of deep despair because of her social isolation. Her ability to form trusting relationships was badly damaged and she felt her loneliness keenly. From time to time she would become suicidal. When asked what she believed would happen if she died, she replied, 'I could be with God and be his helper in looking after the human race.' For her this seemed easier than coming close to a living person.

Usually, however, when people are able to work with the therapeutic process they are also able to work on ways in which their own projections become involved in their beliefs and practice. By looking at themselves they are able to see what they are putting on to God and own it as part of their own psyche, increasingly allowing God to be other. To be seeking God is to be subject to illusions and fantasies at least some of which we have to learn to let go. As a person comes to terms with a counsellor's refusal to rescue or to intervene, alongside their willingness to stay with a situation, it may also become possible to relinquish a God who is on tap to put everything right. In cases of particularly challenging differences of belief, the counsellor has the hard task of trying to discern where a psychological interpretation falls short of respect for the client. It is always possible that the other person is in touch with something which is simply inaccessible to the counsellor, and it may not be the counsellor's place to judge the validity of that experience.

A fundamental resource

When people talk about prayer they often describe it as both essential and precious. It provides containment at times which would otherwise be impossibly difficult. For counsellors, far from being seen as an uncalled-for intervention, it can make it possible to tolerate the non-intervention which is required in order to allow others to grow into their own paths. Prayer is seen as nourishment, being fed, an extra reserve. One counsellor described it as the most important and fundamental resource he possessed as a human being. 'Without prayer,' said another, 'without God, I'd be dead.'

3
Praying for others: pitfalls, dilemmas and quick fixes

'One image of prayer is the artist, who, rejecting easy false mediocre forms and hoping for the right thing, the best thing, *waits*. This too is an image . . . of all kinds of stilled attentive situations in work and in human relations where the waiting is intensely collected yet relaxed: "fearlessly passive" to use Adorno's phrase.'

(Iris Murdoch: *Metaphysics as a Guide to Morals*)[1]

Although the word 'prayer' is one which many people shy away from because of the beliefs it may imply, something of what is involved is perhaps accessible even to those who do not believe in a personal God, in the appreciation of beauty, of creativity, or of a quality of attention to our surroundings which is vigilant and respectful. It is possible to meditate on these things or contemplate them deeply without taking on the baggage of a particular religious faith. This is not the same thing as prayer, which, as we have seen, involves dialogue with an 'other', but a particular quality of attention is common to both.

Sooner or later, however, the question arises, 'What does it mean to pray for someone or something?' This is something that many people instinctively do at times of crisis. In *The*

Archers, recently, one of the characters was rushed into hospital. The episode ended with her husband saying, 'Please, God, let her be all right.' Prayer for other people, for peace, for the good of the world and so on is also one of the fundamental aspects of prayer. Again, it is never simply a matter of one's own private relationship with God; prayer always takes us into relationship with others. Very often, people are asked to pray for someone or something in particular – what does this mean?

Being asked to pray

Requests to pray come in various forms. A friend might say, 'Please pray for me because . . .', and although what one actually does in response to that will depend on one's particular understanding of prayer, this is a relatively straightforward situation. Often, requests for prayer come from people who do not themselves pray or even believe in God: 'Next time you go to church, could you light a candle for x [a mutual friend], who is ill' is an interesting request when it comes from someone who would not pray themselves. I am happy to comply, but also intrigued as to what the person who asks this is actually saying. One possibility is, 'I'm not sure if I believe, but since you do, perhaps you can do something.' This, again, highlights the communal aspect of prayer. Even those who do pray have times when it is difficult or impossible to do so, and may then draw strength from the fact that prayer is going on, even if they do not feel able to take part in it themselves. In this sense, whenever we pray, we are praying for each other: our prayer, though uniquely our own, also belongs to everybody.

A call to prayer can be experienced in less direct ways. One young priest was perturbed by what seemed to be a kind of sixth sense, by which she sometimes knew things about people without being told. A disturbing example of this occurred when she was introduced to someone, and knew immediately, 'You are going to die soon.' The prediction turned out to be correct, even though neither the man nor his family knew he was ill at the time. As often happens in situations like this, the priest was left with a feeling of guilt, almost as though she had somehow contributed to the man's death by knowing about it. She began to treat such experiences as promptings to pray for the people involved. In this way she was able to make use of her intuitions as a gift – even though a difficult one – rather than feeling drawn into something disturbing and 'spooky'. Again some people will turn to prayer as a matter of course when they hear bad news about someone, or find themselves unable to help someone in trouble in any practical way.

Many would agree that this is an appropriate thing to do, though they might see the purpose of prayer differently. There are many instances where individuals have been critically ill or injured and others have prayed for them and they have recovered. Because of this people sometimes form prayer networks which can be called upon to pray if there is a particular crisis. For every one of these examples, however, there are others where the same has happened and the person has not recovered. We often do not know how, if at all, a person may have been affected by prayer, and some would argue that the primary purpose of prayer is not visible recovery so much as inner healing. As is often the case with counselling, there may be no change that can be observed or measured, but those directly involved will feel that something significant has taken place.

With the coming of the Internet, it is not unusual to receive a round-robin email asking for prayer for a complete stranger who is in some kind of crisis. Some welcome this, and would see it as quite natural to pray for anyone in distress, whether or not they are personally known to them; it is a means of surrounding a person with as much prayer as possible. Others find it difficult to know how to respond. 'I've always found it extremely difficult to pray for people or situations that I don't know,' said an Anglican minister who had also trained as a counsellor. 'It is extremely difficult if I don't feel involved with a person.' A Jewish woman whose mother was dying struggled to understand what it meant that her father sent a letter asking for prayer to an orthodox group who did not know her mother. 'It didn't make any sense to me – none at all. They didn't know her, so what place would they do it from?' She went on to say that she thought praying for somebody was a sort of threesome, involving you, God and your friend. Another woman, a devout Roman Catholic, called a priest to her dying mother. Neither of them knew the priest, and she found the experience all but unbearable: 'There was this stranger babbling over my mother, and I wondered what we were doing.'

Again, for every story of this kind, there are others which testify to the prayer of strangers. Irina Ratushinskaya, a Russian poet imprisoned by the Soviets, describes in one of her poems how she was helped to endure extreme conditions by an awareness that 'someone is praying for me now'.[2] It seemed that the prayer somehow reached her, like 'a resounding note of love.' When Rabbi Lionel Blue had major heart surgery a few years ago, he came back to the *Today* programme on Radio Four, and described how amongst all the dread immediately prior to the operation, he had been surprised to find himself bathed in a powerful sense of being loved and cared for. Suddenly it came to him that these were the prayers of his listeners, which he had asked for without really thinking what was implied. It was only in the experience that he realised what he had asked, and thanked the many strangers who had provided it.

Some years ago when my husband was critically ill, I asked the nuns at a convent to pray for him. Again, I did not really have a clear idea of what I meant, especially as they did not know my husband. I also rang a friend with the same request, and he surprised me by demonstrating prayer in action; he appeared in intensive care at midnight with supplies of sandwiches and chocolate. Eventually I went home and tried to pray myself, but after a while it became clear that it was time to get some sleep. It was not that prayer had become unnecessary, but it was going on anyway, and it seemed that it was somehow being taken care of by the sisters at the convent. My husband recovered, and a few days later I joined them for the Eucharist, where for the first time I noticed the naming of people during the intercessions. This was at a time when my relationship with any kind of 'church' was highly exploratory and I was instinctively annoyed, because it reminded me of services in my childhood where I had found such lists of names dreary and meaningless. At that moment I also realised that they were doing the very thing I had asked them to do a few days previously, and which had seemed so powerful. 'Is that all they do?' I asked myself. Eventually it seemed to me that the answer was both yes and no: that may be the only time a person is named, but the naming takes place in a context of constant prayer, where the veil is already thin.

From time to time there have been rather strange experiments to try to find out whether prayer is worthwhile. One of the most bizarre was a survey carried out in the 1940s to test the hypothesis that since the Royal Family were prayed for at every service of the Church of England, they were more prayed for than anyone else and therefore ought to be healthier and live longer. A survey covering several centuries demonstrated that they nevertheless had shorter lives on average than most people, and it was therefore concluded that prayer was not effective.

Perhaps even more absurd was the work of psychologists in the 1960s who set up a controlled experiment with three groups of plants. All were given the same physical care, but one group was 'prayed for' that they would flourish, another that they would not flourish, and the third was not prayed for at all. Both the first two groups did better than the third. It does not seem we can conclude much from such experiments, except perhaps that any attention is better than none, a conclusion which is borne out in many different situations. Research on US soldiers in Vietnam showed that men who were injured survived on average twice as long if they were not alone in their foxholes, than if they were. Companionship can take strange forms, however: even negative attention driven by anger, hatred or revenge can stimulate a certain instinct to win or to survive, as witnessed by much prison literature. Experiments like those described above, however, do not tell us much about prayer, or praying for others, and this is hardly surprising, since prayer is not a magic formula to bring about predetermined results. Prayer is no more and no less than an encounter with God.

Praying for others: a three-sided relationship

A counsellor who practised in a church context described how she prayed every day alone at home for a number of people who came to her for counselling. She kept a list of these people so that she would remember them all in her prayers, and saw this as part of her work. One day she was trying to pray for the people on her list, all of whom were in various forms of difficulty or distress, when she realised to her horror that she was bored. This made her feel terribly guilty, since these were all people she knew well and cared about, or so she had thought. As we talked, it turned out that she was overwhelmed by the sheer emotional weight of the list of names, each of which represented a wealth of problems. It seemed she would never get through it, and all of it depressed her, as well it might. I asked her what she was trying to do when she prayed for these people and she said that she was trying to bring them before God, so that God could heal them. 'And where is God?' I asked. 'I don't know,' she replied.

Exploring this further she found that the list had taken over from what had previously been a dialogue between herself and God. It was as though she was at the meeting point of two lines which went off in different directions. In one direction was God; in the other was the people on the list. When she tried to pray for them she felt trapped in their pain, and cut off from God. 'What about them?' I asked. 'Do they have any connection to God?' 'Yes,' she replied, 'but I think I had forgotten about that. There is a third line, making a triangle which joins them to God.' 'And what is happening when you try to pray?' She eventually decided that concentrating too hard on the list collapsed the triangle, so that all that was left was a horizontal line between her and the others, and God was somewhere else altogether. She became so caught up in their troubles, that she lost contact with the prayer relationship she usually found sustaining. If, however, she were able to stand back a little, and allow the triangle to open out, she could keep in her awareness both God and the people she was praying for. In this way, she was not so much brooding on their difficulties, as allowing herself to stand in God's presence alongside them, knowing that God also loved each one of them in their own right. She could let God take care of his own relationship with them, and make space for her own relationship with him.

People who have discovered how to do this will sometimes say of their prayer for others, 'It was easy', or 'It was no work at all.' At other times, even for the same people, prayer can have a quite passionate element which is more like standing before God and pleading for another person. For example, Metropolitan Anthony of Sourozh describes praying for the dead as having one hand metaphorically on the shoulder of one's departed friend, and the other reaching out to God, reminding God of the good this person did in his or her life.[3] It is not that God does not know about these things, but by entering into this position, the person praying is entering actively into relationship both with the dead person and with God. One might think of it as making the good that person did alive in the world, and so enabling him or her to approach closer to God's presence.

Similarly, in praying for people who are still alive, people often describe themselves as trying to be a channel for healing, helping God's love to reach the other person. A counsellor on his first placement became involved with a suicidal young woman who was very dependent on him, and he had trouble containing his anxiety. He found himself wanting her to be able to receive from God the constant care he himself could not give, since his experience was that many people who turn to God in prayer find that something actually changes. For her, however, God seemed distant and threatening. 'So,' he said, 'I was praying to God that he would somehow make himself real to her.' His desire that she should be able to experience God as loving rather than angry and punitive was very strong. As a Christian he longed to be able to say to her, 'I've had the experience of God making a difference in my life, and I wish you could have it too,' but as a counsellor he felt unable to say this.

Working with this woman was an important experience for him, because up until that time he had kept his religious beliefs and his professional practice separate, thinking of himself as being like a doctor or an engineer, who has a job to do. Now he had to begin to work out for himself how far it was right to continue to keep his beliefs in the background, or whether it was possible to allow them to enter into his work without becoming propagandist.

In any situation where one is praying for someone else, it is important to be able to trust God's love and providence sufficiently to be able to lay aside one's own desires for that person. 'I believe that God will take action,' said one man, 'but I don't feel I should seek to control what that action will be.' Nevertheless, there are times when another person's plight makes us long for things to improve, and it is easy to fall into the trap of either, like the counsellor with the list, becoming unable to find God in the prayer, or alternatively of *interposing* oneself between God and the other person.

An addiction counsellor interviewed a young man who, after many failed attempts, wanted to try again to overcome his alcoholism. In accordance with his usual practice, the counsellor sent the man away to think over whether he was willing to commit himself to the treatment programme on offer. He was very moved by the encounter and found himself praying and pleading to God that the man would take up the treatment, and that it would help him. As he prayed he gradually became aware of the young man's own relationship with God, and that this was something which he, the counsellor, knew nothing about. It might be possible to help him, but he also had to accept, as he put it, that 'as far as his [the young man's] God was concerned, he might have some more drinking to do before the time was right for him.' This did not, of course, mean that he was not prepared to work with him, but it did mean that he was able to enter into the work more freely, in the knowledge that it might fail. 'It's difficult,' he said, 'because you are sort of eager beaver, and you are asking God to direct you, but you are dealing with another human being.'

Counselling is basically concerned with the relationship between two people engaged on a particular task, and people who try in whatever way to combine this with prayer can find themselves in difficulties. Here we will look at some of the pitfalls and dilemmas which people encounter, and at the phenomenon of the 'quick fix'.

Some pitfalls between counselling and prayer

A particularly hazardous area is using prayer within the counselling session itself. Sometimes a client will ask a counsellor to pray with him or with her, and this may be something quite different from the kind of relationship the counsellor, as a professional, would expect to have. It was not, explained one, that she did not believe in prayer, 'but,' she said, 'I find it difficult to be in those two positions at the same time.' A particular anxiety expressed by many counsellors is that the client may imagine that the counsellor has a special 'hot-line' to God. This can also be very seductive for the counsellor, who may fall into the trap of thinking that the client is not capable of talking to God in his or her own right.

One woman told her counsellor about her painful feelings of envy when she went to church. 'Everyone seems to have an experience of God, except me,' she said. She had seen a counsellor at the church who had prayed with her, and she described the prayer as quite wonderful: very sensitive and fluent. 'And how was the counselling session you had together?' asked her counsellor. 'That was a bit of a waste of time,' replied the client. 'She did not seem to understand what

I was on about.' A few minutes later she asked, 'Why don't you pray with me? It is a way of caring for me.' 'I think you have been telling me,' replied the counsellor, 'that it would be taking away your relationship with God.'

At the very least, anyone who undertakes spoken prayer, whether it is spontaneous or chosen from written prayers, has to take responsibility for what is being said and being heard in the name of God. There are situations where this is entirely appropriate. In the rite of confession or reconciliation, for example, a priest may give advice and pray in a way that is related to what has been said, but the content of the confession remains 'under the seal'. The priest is not at liberty to repeat it or even to refer back to it with that person outside the context of the sacrament. What has been said by the priest, however, is understood as emerging from his or her state of prayer while hearing the confession, and to be spoken in the capacity of guide and helper. The proper focus is not a dialogue between two people but an unburdening to God, of which the priest is witness. In the Orthodox tradition this is symbolised by confession taking place in front of the icon of Christ, with the priest standing to one side.

Although a counselling session may in some sense be confessional, it is not explicitly prayerful in this sense, nor is it the counsellor's role to be a spiritual guide for the client. It is for this reason that requests for prayer are often refused. People can sometimes define what they do in strange ways. 'I never pray with clients during the session,' declared one counsellor, so I was surprised when a little later on she referred to praying with a client. 'But I thought you didn't do that,' I said. 'I don't,' she replied. 'We have a short period of prayer, then we have the session, then we end with another prayer.' I asked if her clients were aware that this was what they were doing, and she realised that perhaps she needed to clarify the situation both for herself and for them.

Even when it is not brought into the session, prayer can cross boundaries in a way that is not necessarily appropriate to the counselling situation. Many churchgoers share intercession times when anyone is free to name particular people in need of prayer. Once when I was ill, I cancelled a meeting with a colleague, but as I was working the following day, my clients did not know, or need to know, that I had not been well. One of them, however, phoned to ask if she should come to our appointment. I was surprised by the question and asked her why she had phoned. It turned out she had been at a service the other side of town where my colleague had prayed aloud for me among other people who were ill, and she thought she perhaps should not come if it was going to be too much for me. Although touched by my colleague's concern, I felt irritated, as though my personal privacy and my work space had been invaded, even if the incident did provide valuable clues as to the state of the relationship with the client.

Some dilemmas

Mixing religious faith and counselling can generate anxiety about whether one is being sufficiently professional. A counsellor who had worked over a long period with a married couple who eventually resolved their difficulties was very moved by what had happened in their work together. She felt that they had struggled hard, and shown her something that gave her hope. When they said goodbye at the end of the last session she found herself saying, 'God bless you,' and then felt extremely anxious that she had let her professional boundaries slip.

Again, a Jungian therapist, who is used to working with myth and fairy tale, told a client a Christian legend from her own faith tradition which she had herself found helpful. Afterwards she wondered whether she had overstepped the boundaries between her personal faith and her professional role.

Two people who had been in counselling as clients gave different responses to this dilemma. The first had been converted to Christianity after she had finished counselling, but she knew that her counsellor was a Christian. 'When I discovered all the richness that she was in touch with all that time,' she said, 'I was furious that she hadn't shared it with me. I realise she couldn't, professionally, but it seemed such a waste, because I realised that this was what she believed in that made her such a fantastic person. It was what sustained her. The other stuff – myths and so on – are really helpful, but they are not what anyone lives by these days.' The other, an agnostic, affirmed the anxiety. 'It would come too close,' she said, 'if someone told me a Christian story. I could relate to the story of Demeter and Persephone because it was far enough away. But a Christian story – we say with our lips that these are just myth, but do we really believe that? I would feel somehow judged if someone did that to me.'

Another source of anxiety is that for the counsellor, as well as for the client, life is an ongoing journey, in which significant events – illness, bereavement, changes in relationships, etc. – continue to happen, and these may affect their religious faith. There may be times when a counsellor faces a crisis of faith and prayer becomes difficult. One man described how he had found it very hard to keep going at a time when he was unable to experience the presence of God, which up to that time had always sustained him in his work. 'I've always been able to carry on,' he said, 'because there was a sense that God was there with me and I felt his presence. This time I didn't. It was just absent. And that was very, very frightening, because you begin to feel it will never come back again.'

For this reason counsellors may be wary of mixing their religious practice with their work. 'I don't know where I am with it all,' said one, 'so I'd rather not involve anyone else in my muddle.' Since the process of training as a counsellor and the psychological exploration that goes with it often bring about deep questioning of religious belief and practice, many counsellors become anxious about what they do believe, and whether they themselves are deluded. In order to counteract this, some people will choose a supervisor whom they know to have different beliefs, in order to provide a counterbalance and to keep their work within a psychological framework. One counsellor who had started out by keeping the two areas of his life quite separate, nevertheless became concerned about whether this could actually be done. On the one hand he was committed to the idea that counselling was not about converting people to any particular belief. On the other his life was based on his own belief that God was revealed historically and uniquely through the life of Jesus of Nazareth, because he was God in human form. 'Attention has to be paid to that revelation,' he said. 'It has to be taken seriously.' By leaving this aspect out of his work he felt he was blocking off a very important reality.

Something of this anxiety was experienced by a Christian counsellor who worked with a couple involved in pagan practices. Hearing what went on in the rites they took part in made her very uncomfortable. She prayed internally, saying, 'I need anchoring so that I am not seeing the wrong thing here because my beliefs are different.' She eventually concluded that what the couple were doing was healthy in terms of their relationship, and that that was after all the aspect of their lives with which she was being asked to work, but it was something of a struggle to maintain the objectivity of her professional role.

Clients, on the other hand, may be reluctant to enter into counselling in case it affects their life and relationships in ways that they see as incompatible with their religious beliefs. After a few sessions, a client and I had to decide whether to continue working together. Her life situation was painful, and prayer was important to her in living through it. According to my clinical judgement, she was being made ill by fear of her own anger which she had suppressed over a lifetime, and which was by now making it very hard for her to function. She was finding our sessions helpful, but one of her reservations about continuing was, 'I don't want to become the kind of person who only cares about their own happiness.' For her, this was a very real difficulty. She was afraid that if she went on, and allowed too many of her feelings to emerge, she would lose her ability to function in her family in the way she considered right.

There are various ways in which her statement could be interpreted from a psychological point of view. Perhaps it expressed buried anger against people in her life who had only considered their own happiness and not hers. It might also say something about how she perceived me as a counsellor. If she continued would she become more like me, and to what extent was I the sort of person who put my own happiness before everything else? These might well be themes that required exploring. At the same time, while the psychological implications were fairly clear and available to be worked with, there was a real challenge to me as counsellor about the nature of our work together and how that related to her way of life as a Christian.

In some ways it can be more difficult for someone who shares the belief and practice of the client to respond to these questions, since he or she may also be facing similar dilemmas. On the other hand, someone who does not share the experience of prayer and how it can affect decisions and ways of living, might see these anxieties as something imposed on the client by others, and find it difficult to understand just how real these concerns may be to the individual.

Where counsellor and client do share the same faith, they may believe very different things about what God is like. Most of the relationships discussed in counselling are with people the counsellor never meets (a different situation, for example, from that of a minister engaged in pastoral work within his or her own community). How is a counsellor to react when he or she hears God described in terms which are alien to his or her own experience? Does the contract allow for discussion or challenge?

As she left at the end of a session, one woman asked her counsellor to pray for her during the week, which the counsellor agreed to do. It seemed to her that the client was expressing a shared trust in God and in the value of prayer. She remembered the client by name during her prayer time, without there being any particular content to the prayer. A few weeks later, however, she discovered that the client meant something far more specific. They were working on family problems which the counsellor saw from a psychological point of view; she was trying to help her client understand the role of family dynamics in her difficulties. As far as the client was concerned, however, these difficulties were the result of demonic attack, and she wanted the counsellor, by praying, to enter into battle against these demons. The counsellor was perturbed because, rather than protect the client, she was wanting her to face what was going on and look at ways in which she herself could bring about change. She began to wonder if by asking for her prayers the client was avoiding inner work which needed to be done on a psychological level: in effect passing the problem back to the counsellor. On the other hand, she did not see it as her role to question the client's beliefs. They did not have any delusional character; they were simply based in a different Christian tradition from that to which the counsellor belonged, and it did not seem to her that she had any right to judge their validity. Nevertheless, it made it difficult for her to pursue the psychological angle, which she felt was never really tackled in their work together.

Aware of such difficulties, some counsellors refuse to pray with their clients or to be drawn into agreeing to pray for them. 'If clients want me to pray or want to be prayed for,' said one counsellor, 'they don't need to come to me because that is not what I am there for.' Too much is at stake, it is felt, in terms of mistaken assumptions, or a false reliance on prayer to sidestep the psychological work.

Yet, for counsellors and clients for whom prayer is an important part of their lives, it can seem perverse to try to shut this out from the work they do together. Although they might not talk about it in their sessions, counsellors and clients often pray for each other between times. This may be especially true when difficult work is going on and the relationship between them is deepening, stirring up feelings that are hard to tolerate or to understand. Some find this helpful, but it probably requires the person praying to be prepared not to prejudge the outcome. Often what is needed is for both parties to the relationship to become more aware of what their own contribution is to the problem, so that they are not, by asking God to put things right, avoiding looking at changes they themselves need to make.

A counsellor described a relationship with a client which she found difficult because, although she had great sympathy for this person's problems, she was also finding her increasingly irritating. She took this to supervision, where she identified aspects of the client which reminded her of her own mother, with whom she had a difficult relationship. This helped her to discern more clearly what was her own personal response and what it was in the client's behaviour that needed to be challenged. In technical terms, she had identified the 'counter-transference': reactions in the counsellor to the client, where the client has touched on something in the counsellor's unconscious. If the counsellor can work with that, it can enable a more open approach to the client, and also provide clues as to what is not being said in the session.

A few weeks later, however, she described how she had also taken the situation into her prayer. 'I was meditating on my relationship with x,' she said, 'and I realised that whatever was going on in the counter-transference, my own failure of compassion was making a barrier between us. I was finding it difficult to challenge her because I could not do so calmly and without turning critical. But now I can.' Asked what had changed, she replied, 'I was thinking about x and me, and I had been struggling with the fact that God loved her as much as he loved me and I was finding it hard to accept this. And then I realised that God went on loving me even though I was feeling so negative about x. That made it difficult to feel so critical of her. Before that I was more concerned that she should change, not me.'

Avoiding the 'quick fix'

The reason some counsellors give for not mixing prayer with their work is that they are wary of the 'quick fix' assumption: that God will miraculously solve the problem if they pray. It can be very tempting to assume that prayer can bypass the painful emotional work of counselling. The situation is different from one where a person might ask a priest or spiritual director to pray because that is part of their agreed role. Many counsellors feel that it is important to differentiate between this and the work that they are trying to do. A client who begins by asking a counsellor to pray, may in effect be saying: 'I find these sessions uncomfortable and would rather we ask God to put it right than put ourselves through the pain of talking about it.'

A member of a personal growth group which I facilitated was extremely reluctant to engage with the sharing of experience that was the task of the group. Eventually other members found her silence uncomfortable and somebody asked her what was going on. She replied, 'I hate these groups, so I sit here and pray until it is all over.' In another group which began each session with prayer, one member prayed aloud that we would all get on well together, making it very difficult for other members to return to difficult interpersonal issues which had arisen the week before.

This can also happen in individual sessions. A client who begins the session with prayer may well say something like: 'Bless our work today and enable [the counsellor] to help me.' This can put pressure on the counsellor to act in a way that the client perceives as helpful, which may not necessarily be the best way forward. Since this has been spoken as a prayer, the counsellor may not feel able to address what the client has said, whereas if it had been said directly it would be valuable material to work with.

A student who was going through a painful bereavement told his counsellor: 'People say God is suffering with me. And I think: "Thanks a lot, God. How about doing something a bit more constructive?" ' The counsellor, who was inexperienced and eager to help, referred him to some tapes on suffering which she had found useful. She herself had no problem with this, but her supervisor picked up on it when they were talking about the session. She thought the counsellor had missed a valuable opportunity to help the client explore the feelings that lay behind what he had said. The counsellor, on the other hand, argued that the student's protest about God's lack of positive help was his way of praying at that time. She was meeting him on common ground, by acknowledging that there was a problem with which she, too, had needed help. By making an interpretation or probing the underlying emotions, she continued, she might be failing to take seriously the spiritual dimension which was very real to him. As far as the supervisor was concerned, however, it was not the counsellor's task to attempt to shore up the client's religious faith. By offering the tapes she had avoided the client's pain, and she urged the counsellor to look more closely at her own reactions to grief, and why she might have needed to do this.

This situation touches on a core problem about mutuality in the counselling relationship which often comes up when people are combining counselling practice with some kind of pastoral role. It is often argued, particularly by people who work in a pastoral context, that coming alongside another is more a matter of sharing human frailty than probing other people's wounds. We are all in need of help, and sometimes it can be useful to share what we ourselves have found helpful; it can be a source of hope. There is no doubt that counsellors sometimes do this at the level of strategy. They may, for example, encourage a client to write a journal, or analyse their dreams in particular ways, or tease out what they are thinking about themselves and challenge it.

Nevertheless, such interventions need to be treated very sparingly, and with a keen sense of timing. Especially when it comes to matters of faith, there is a strong argument against being too explicit. Each of us has to find our own path to God, and there are places outside the counselling room that are appropriate to this search. Although both counsellor and supervisor in this particular situation were committed Christians, they had quite different views about what should take place in the session. The counsellor's focus was on offering positive help, since the client was floundering in his relationship with God. The supervisor believed that if the client were met at a level which released and helped him manage his feelings, holding back from 'God-talk', he would ultimately find a more authentic spiritual path. This might turn out to be quite different from either hers or the counsellor's, but that was not directly their concern.

When a counsellor has a strong faith, it can be difficult to hold back from interventions which appear to point the way to something valuable, but there is a danger of imposing something on the client without really entering into his or her emotional problems. Many people would see it as stepping outside the counselling contract, which is not essentially concerned with religious faith. It is for this kind of reason that most people who are experienced in both counselling and spiritual guidance tend to keep them as separate disciplines, being clear about which role they are taking with a particular person.

In all these pitfalls and dilemmas there seems to be a central difficulty in clarifying what belongs in prayer and what belongs in the counselling relationship. How one answers this will depend partly on one's view of what prayer is, and what it is for. There is an argument that one can only go so far on a human level; true healing comes only from God, and, as in the inscription above the door to Jung's house: 'Bidden or not bidden God is present.' Therefore, the two cannot be separated. There is also, however, a kind of 'prudent compartmentalisation' which says that working on the level of human relationships is risky enough. We can acquire a certain expertise, and this is what clients come to counsellors for. If they are seeking spiritual guidance, they should go to someone experienced in this.

It is often easier to retain an open mind psychologically than in relation to prayer, which can have such a profound effect on one's life that one develops very strong beliefs about what it is. Yet, since prayer is an ongoing encounter with someone who can never fully be known, these may change significantly over a lifetime. At the very least, we can be dramatically surprised.

A priest was in charge of a community for the mentally ill who lived very closely together. It became something of a joke in the community that he had a longing for a clavichord, and one of the boys who lived there took this on as a subject of prayer. He prayed incessantly for the clavichord, in spite of complaints from the other residents. 'Please stop him,' they would say, 'we can't stand him going on day and night in the chapel.' The priest talked with the boy, and told him that prayer did not work like this. On the priest's birthday a large postbag arrived, much of it cards from friends and members of the community saying things like 'Wot, no clavichord?' Afterwards he turned to the heap of dull brown envelopes and bills he had put to one side. The top one of these was a letter from a complete stranger wondering if a clavichord he was getting rid of would be of use to the community. The boy was delighted, the priest dumbfounded. 'But,' he said, 'in the manner of these things, when it eventually arrived it was not a very good clavichord.'

4

Why pray? Prayer and the counselling relationship working together

'The psalms are to prayer,' said a priest who is also a musician, 'as Bach is to music.' What he had in mind was that by studying and using the psalms we can find out what prayer is, just as students of harmony and counterpoint may take Bach chorales and fugues as a model of how music is constructed. If we read the psalms we find many different elements of a relationship, a relationship with God which expresses a whole range of human emotions. They cry out to God from the depths of desolation, and praise him with a vital delight in creation. They protest at the ways of the world, and vent anger for wrongs done. They complain of long periods of waiting for something to come right; they express a deep trust in God to be constant through devastating hardship and affliction. They talk of despair – all the clinical symptoms of depression can be found in the psalms – of grief, and of restoration. And they tell the history of the Jewish people through wars and exile, going over these stories, trying to make sense of them. Throughout we find the psalmist moving from sadness, desolation and anger to an equally powerful joy and trust in ultimate goodness. Often this happens with no explanation; it appears to be simply part of the relationship.

All these aspects of a relationship with God are found in descriptions of prayer to the present day. They also resonate strongly with what goes on in counselling, when counsellor and client grapple with their reactions to each other in the privacy of the sessions, to the stories that are told, and how those stories relate to the situations in which they live. Whether the focus is spiritual, as in prayer, or psychological, as in counselling, a journey into the unknown is involved. To undertake this journey, it is essential to set time aside, alone or with one or more companions, but the process is working if what takes place within that secluded space has consequences in the outside world. While some kind of withdrawal is necessary, this is not an end in itself, but a means to living more fully. The carefully guarded boundaries of counselling can be compared with a deliberate retreat from everyday life for spiritual purposes.

The latter kind of withdrawal began to be important in the life of Christians in the fourth century, a time when the major persecutions were over, and Christianity had become the established religion of the Roman Empire. The first Christian monastics went out to live in the desert, and saw this as a way of coming to grips with a deep level of reality which was masked by life in the cities. Their aim was to meet the forces of evil head on, and they believed that through their struggles in prayer and self-denial they were fighting a battle on behalf of the rest of humanity. It is also on this basis that some people today feel called to abandon ordinary everyday living for some form of 'desert', whether for a few days' retreat, or as a way of life.

Similarly, perhaps, many of those who take up counselling as a profession do so because they themselves have discovered new depth and liberation through undertaking an inner journey. Having developed a greater emotional flexibility, they are able to help others process some of those things which, undigested, may be physically or mentally damaging. Marie-Louise von Franz, a disciple of Jung, drew the comparison directly:

> I think our way [of getting in touch with unknown
> parts of ourselves] imposes a kind of discipline on all
> individuals which has an analogy in the monastic life . . .
> For instance, remaining with the difficulty for a long
> time, giving up other occupations in order to have
> enough time and energy for this main problem,
> practicing a kind of asceticism.[1]

It is for this reason that counselling sessions take place in a
carefully protected space – a different form, perhaps, of the
desert – in order to make it possible to pursue a particular
kind of inner work.

At the same time, there are specific elements of the spiritual
search, and of prayer itself, which seem to have a direct
bearing on the counselling process. Three of these will be
explored here: seeing light in darkness, alone or with others;
finding nourishment; and discovering in ancient traditions
resonances with our own lives which give us a sense of connection with humanity at large.

Seeking the light in darkness: alone or with others

For many people, prayer arises from an experience of intense
loneliness, as described by the writer of this letter:

> To me, being a foreigner in this land and in general
> often feeling a stranger to humankind and life, praying
> starts with a bewildering feeling of being alone in an
> overwhelming lack of understanding and loss of love.
> You psychologists have terms for this, and those are
> not what I mean. Still, I can pray best when I feel
> broken-hearted. I ask for someone's solid, loving,
> reliable, eternal understanding and guidance. We hanker
> after sense and structure when the world seems too
> chaotic and perverse. So it brings peace to turn to God
> and hand over ourselves and we feel his presence,
> which we know to be beyond our brains . . . I often
> wonder if other people feel so utterly lonely that they
> can only pray to God, or am I mad?

People are often drawn to pray in this way, through brokenness or emptiness, which in turn may lead to an experience of a presence which they call God. A Quaker, James Nayler, who died in Bridewell prison in 1660, wrote of it like this:

> There is a Spirit which I feel that delights to do no evil, nor to revenge any wrong, but delights to endure all things in hope to enjoy its own in the end . . . for its ground and spring is the mercies and forgiveness of God . . . I found it alone, being forsaken.[2]

For some people, then, experience of such a presence arises when the ordinary supports of everyday life are stripped away, something which often happens in spite of ourselves, when the things or people on whom we normally rely abandon us or are lost. It may also be a deliberate step, which carries particular risks: modern retreatants and contemplatives, like their earlier role models, can find they become very vulnerable. Indeed, this is often the experience of busy people who take a holiday. When we leave behind our ordinary lives for somewhere quiet, all sorts of difficulties may emerge. Memories surface, or aspects of ourselves which we find unacceptable; or a depression sets in, which may be protecting us from traumatic memories or feelings which have previously been repressed.

Repression in this sense means a process whereby an experience which is beyond our emotional capacity becomes forgotten: it is inaccessible to the conscious mind. It may remain that way for ever, but it may also express itself in mental or physical symptoms, or emerge spontaneously. The latter tends to happen either when something occurs which makes us more vulnerable, such as a major life change, or at a time when life has become settled, and the psyche seems almost to make a decision that it is now safe to confront what went on. A similar phenomenon may be found between the generations. It may be impossible for someone who has suffered extreme trauma ever to face the memory; but those memories, and the feelings which go with them, may be processed by the second or third generation, through the stories that have been passed on.

Something similar to what happens when we withdraw from daily life can also happen when we enter into the seclusion of a counselling relationship. It is part of the task of the counsellor to help clients get in touch with their feelings. Often, this releases intense emotions: distress, need, rage, shame or grief; or memories that are hard to name or to endure. This can put great pressure on a counsellor to intervene, to rescue the client, and one of the things which counsellors have to learn is to hold back. Particularly in the early stages, they can be shocked to find that they are being told by supervisors not to intervene or to comfort, or at least not in any immediate or obvious way. The natural human instinct is to find some concrete way to help, but by learning to sit this kind of experience out, they may come to find that something else is in play. 'There is sometimes a spiritual happening or a moment which is understood,' said one. 'It is not prayer in the traditional sense, and some people might say it is a cop-out, but I experience it. Because I can't put it on paper or do research about it doesn't mean to say it doesn't exist.'

Another counsellor went further in defining this kind of experience as prayer. He was sitting with a young woman who was on the verge of breakdown, and was struggling to hold back because he knew that any intervention would be futile. 'So,' he said, 'there is no alternative but to pray.' Prayer meant trying to empty himself of his need and desire to help while remaining attentive and vigilant: 'the mind at rest, but waked and on guard', as he put it. In psychological terms he was communicating to the young woman that someone was with her, and able to stay with her where she was without fear, rather than trying to sort out her problems. He could do this because of a basic confidence, as he put it, in the trustworthiness of being. 'What often prevents people from feeling better about themselves,' he said, 'is a failure of nerve.'

For him, however, what he was doing was also prayer,

is defined, is never made in isolation. It is frequently insisted on. Basil the Great, a fourth-century bishop and monastic founder, warned his monks: 'If anyone claims to be able to be completely self-sufficient, to be capable of reaching perfection without anyone else's help . . . he is just like someone trying to practise the trade of a carpenter without touching wood.'³ Again, John of the Ladder, a seventh-century monk, insisted that the love of God and the love of one's fellow human beings cannot be separated: 'Love in its nature makes a human being like God as far as is possible for a human being . . . Love is the complete repudiation of any unkind thought about one's neighbour . . . One who loves God also loves his brother or sister. Indeed the second love is proof of the first.'⁴

It is not surprising, then, that while many people begin to seek God from a position of isolation or loss, for others this journey begins through relationships. One young man, for example, had been brought up to pray every day. When he left home, he began to wonder whether it was just a habit. 'Do I want this in my life or not?' he asked himself. 'Is it something I just do like cleaning my teeth or brushing my hair?' He decided to stop praying, and did not take it up again even though he missed it. In due course, seeking help for a psychological problem, he joined a group which prayed as part of its therapeutic work, and found in this shared prayer something new that had been missing before. 'It gave me something tangible. Somehow my God didn't seem so elusive, so unreachable.' Prayer subsequently became central in his life, both as an individual and as a church member.

Another man, who had been through a particularly traumatic time, went on a long walking holiday to recover. He kept getting the feeling that he was not alone, but whenever he checked, there really was nobody around in the countryside. 'Maybe it's God, then,' he thought idly, and gradually this idea took hold. 'All right, then,' he said, 'if it is you, give me some sort of sign.' That evening he arrived in a village where everything was closed and there was no accommodation. At something of a loss, he knocked on a door at random. The house turned out to be occupied by the village priest, who not only fed him and gave him a bed for the night, but also sent him off the next morning with food for the day's journey. It was only in the morning that he realised that the priest had given up his own bed and slept on the sofa. This generous and unexpected hospitality he took as the sign he had been asking for.

In counselling, it can sometimes seem that people are unable to connect with the God they believe in because they are unable to connect with those around them. If there is little or no experience of love between human beings, or that love has been severely damaged in some way, it can be all but impossible to develop a sense of divine love. (This is the opposite problem from the young woman described in Chapter 2 who found it hard to make relationships and therefore assumed that her *only* loving relationship was with God himself.) One counsellor described this as the basis of her work. She did not directly discuss spiritual concerns with her clients, 'but,' she said, 'what we are doing is incarnating God's love so that people can feel it and use it. Too often they feel cut off from God because they have had no experience of love.' Members of praying communities, like the young man quoted above, have had similar experiences: that it is in *not* being forsaken, but through community, friendship and shared worship that they experience the love that they call God.

As a client, to find oneself accepted without being judged can be an extremely complex and uncomfortable experience. It stirs up deeply buried responses to past failures of care (this, broadly, is a major aspect of what is meant by the transference). One woman, for example, found it extremely difficult to enter into committed relationships because she always expected them to result in loss or betrayal. It was better not to get involved in the first place. She entered into weekly counselling, and after several months she found that she began to trust her counsellor in a way that seemed entirely new to her. That trust brought with it, however, extreme anxiety, since so much depended on it. Her sense of separation from the counsellor between sessions was all but unbearable, every week having to be negotiated as though it lasted a lifetime. When this woman was three years old, her mother had been admitted to hospital. A few days later the mother came home, but she was utterly changed; she had fallen into the grip of a deep depression which continued to affect her throughout her life. For the child, it had been as though her mother had suddenly disappeared, and she now found it hard to believe that the counsellor would not do likewise. While the consistency of the relationship had enabled her to form a deep and trusting attachment, it also brought into consciousness the buried feelings that had been generated by her mother's illness when she was small. She found it extremely hard to maintain her trust when she was not actually with her counsellor. It was as though her very survival was at stake even during a separation of a few days.

One evening, with three days to go before the next session, she was trying to talk herself out of her anxiety, but with little success. However hard she tried to convince herself that she was safe, she felt as though she was falling into endless space. Then something changed. Although she was falling, it seemed to her that something caught her and that, after all, she would not disappear into the void. At the next session she told this to her counsellor and thanked her: 'I think you must have been praying for me,' she added. 'How do you know it was me?' said the counsellor. 'Maybe it was God.' For the client this was a turning point emotionally and spiritually. Psychologically, the process was working; she was internalising the counsellor sufficiently to begin to trust herself to survive separations. That is, an experience of a trusting relationship which could survive separations was helping her to find in herself the capacity for nurture. The external reality – the counsellor – was connecting with and nourishing an internal reality which thereby became part of the client's conscious inner world, and therefore available for use.

At the same time, whatever the counsellor meant by what

she said, the client heard it as: 'I'm only a bit part player in this. It is God who is caring for you.' From that time she named whatever it was that sustained her through her anxiety as God, and when she prayed it was to someone or something who had this quality of safety.

It is also part of the work of counselling that there are inevitable failures of consistency. A counsellor may become ill, or encounter unexpected problems, or at the very least will take holidays. Both the reliability and the failures are important in negotiating a relationship that mirrors what goes on in the outside world. One woman who had great difficulty in sustaining relationships because her trust in others had been badly damaged, was very much helped by working with a well-known therapist whom she saw twice a week for several years. He provided her with a consistent, trustworthy relationship. Later, she went into counselling with someone far less experienced who had not yet organised her practice and her personal life well enough to do this. She (the counsellor) would fail to turn up for sessions, or would cancel them at the last minute on the client's answerphone. 'I learned a lot from that,' said the woman. 'In a way he [the first therapist] was so perfect I couldn't get really angry with him. If I did, I knew it was unjustified – infantile – a kind of play acting. But this woman was really letting me down, so I learned to be really angry.'

In counselling we learn to work with both our separateness and our togetherness. Like the woman who had to overcome her terror of the gaps between sessions we have to learn to trust our own being sufficiently to become ourselves and function as individuals. At the same time counselling often involves discovering that relationships can survive many difficulties, and that we share a great deal with our fellow human beings. A degree of self-sufficiency goes alongside daring to depend on others. 'The loneliness of being our own parent is a Santa Claus tale told by therapists to their clients,' said a group analyst,[5] meaning that once we have come to believe in our own self-sufficiency, we then have to understand that it is not the whole truth. Just as we stop believing in Father Christmas when we reach a certain age, so maturity requires us to accept that as human beings we depend on each other. For counsellors and clients who pray, it is this interdependence among human beings and what it implies about a relationship that both have with the divine that underpins the connection between their prayer and the work.

Finding nourishment: discoveries in silence and emptiness

> . . . I have calmed and quieted my soul,
> like a child quieted at its mother's breast;
> like a child that is quieted is my soul. (Psalm 131:2)

We have already seen that many clients and counsellors find support and nourishment through prayer alongside the work they do together. One way in which counsellors sometimes talk about this, is that prayer helps them to leave behind the work at the end of the day. 'I feel quite confident in leaving them in that holding environment,' said one, 'particularly when I am finding it difficult to be a trustworthy container for what has been told me.' She went on to describe a time when she was working with someone who had been sexually abused, and about whom she was very worried. She was tempted to phone her supervisor to offload some of her anxiety, 'but,' she said, 'I knew that it was crucial that I didn't. The message I had given her [the client] was "I can take whatever you bring". So I knew it was crucial I took it and didn't hand it on to the supervisor. I had three very uncomfortable days.' It was prayer, she said, which enabled her to get through this.

Another counsellor stressed the importance of being grounded in something, and for her the ritual of shared worship in church was crucial to this. 'I've tried to do without,' she said, 'and I can't.' Again, this counsellor had experienced situations in her work which felt simply too big to manage alone: 'You get to the point with some people where it really is on the edge of things between life and death, and I don't personally feel I can hold that without something else.' As she experienced it, there was something real that held both her and her clients, which held the work itself, even though she worked within a framework whereby she never discussed her own beliefs with clients. Sometimes she became anxious that her trust in prayer might be a form of escapism or avoidance, but more strongly she thought it would be foolish to ignore what she saw as an aspect of reality. If all that was involved was oneself, the client, and an abyss into which either or both of you could fall, it was irresponsible, she thought, even to attempt the work. It would mean claiming a degree of power or strength that was simply unrealistic.

She worked for some time with someone who was on the edge of suicide, and who would frequently end sessions by threatening to kill herself as she stormed out. When this happened, the counsellor not only had to deal with her own feelings in response to the attack, but would also be seriously anxious about whether the threat would be carried out. Training and supervision helped her to understand what was going on in terms of psychological theory, and that what the client was doing was a necessary part of working through the problem. When it came to her own survival, however, she felt that the only thing that had kept her going was prayer. For her the central issue was whether this woman would be able to stay in life rather than follow her urge for self-destruction, an urge which took hold when there simply was 'not enough inside herself' to hold together.

The role of prayer in this, as far as the counsellor was concerned, was twofold. There was prayer for the client, that she would somehow be held when her inner world was falling apart, but there was also prayer for herself which gave her some sense of being contained. Paradoxically, this enabled her to let go of the client, not to 'carry her around all the time', which in turn made it easier for her to persist. It seemed to her that there was something continuous or constant at work which was beyond what any human being could provide.

This need not 'to carry the client around all the time' is in itself essential to the counselling process, not only for the well-being of the counsellor, but also for the eventual healing of the client. While a reliable environment facilitates the healing of wounds and the growth of the person, the task of the counsellor is to be, in the words of the psychoanalyst Donald Winnicott, 'good enough'.[6] Winnicott coined this phrase when writing about mothers and babies, and pointed out that the idea of the perfect, all-providing mother is not only impossible to fulfil, but is not in fact in the interests of the child. Inevitably, even the most devoted mother will have other demands on her time, and this is not only realistic, it is also important in order for the child to develop some independence. The child needs to know that his or her needs matter and someone will attend to them, but also needs to learn that the world does not collapse if such attention is not immediately forthcoming. Timing, of course, is crucial. In an ordinary situation of frustration where a baby is left for a short time, she will discover that she can survive and manage her own feelings. If neglect is severe, however, the feelings become unmanageable and trauma takes place. It is in the context of an underlying reliability and continuity that 'failures' or 'forgetting' are necessary in any caring relationship that allows people to grow.

Children naturally experiment with this from an early age, playing at hide-and-seek or disappearing games even before they can walk. It is important to be able to hide and believe one will be found; and that another person can disappear and come back again. This relationship between hiding and finding or being found, between separation and togetherness, is at the very heart of growing up; it also enters into the biblical account of human beings' relationship with God.

In the story of the fall of humankind in Genesis 2–3, Adam and Eve eat the forbidden fruit of the tree of knowledge of good and evil, and this has immediate and dire consequences for human existence. Before they eat this fruit they live in a state of undifferentiated bliss; afterwards they have a new and inescapable awareness. Psychologically, we might describe this as a dawn of consciousness, and the beginnings of taking responsibility for oneself.[7] All at once they become aware of separation: separation from God, and between male and female (Eve is no longer 'bone of my bone and flesh of my flesh' but 'the woman you gave me'). There is a sudden necessity to hide: to hide their bodies behind fig leaves, but also to hide from God. With this comes the ability to lie, something most children develop at the age of around three or four. Overcome with shame, Adam needs to believe he can be forgotten, although of course he is found by God as soon as God comes into the garden, and it immediately becomes obvious that God – and only God – cannot be hidden from or lied to successfully. Their whole relationship to the world is changed; tilling the fields becomes hard labour, and childbirth a painful business. They are evicted from Paradise, and have to fend for themselves. It is God himself, however, who provides Adam and Eve with 'garments of skin' to protect them when he sends them out of the garden.

This is the condition in which we find ourselves as human beings. We are cut off from each other and from the rest of creation; rediscovering our true relationship with other people and with the world can be hard work. In counselling we confront ourselves and discover that our shame can be tolerated; we also learn to live with our separateness, to fend for ourselves. When counselling works, whatever new insights may emerge, it involves a balance between support and withdrawal. By being able to bring the session to an end, and say to herself, 'This is not my problem until next Wednesday at 11 o'clock', a counsellor is not only giving herself a chance to come fresh to the difficulties the next time, but is also putting trust in the client's ability to survive. It also means that she accepts her own limitations: she cannot live the client's life or take it over. She has to stand back sufficiently to allow her clients to find their own way.

In trying to achieve this, a counsellor may find herself in a similar place to that of the letter writer who found prayer out of a sense of emptiness. When the counsellor who was afraid her client might commit suicide prayed, it not only helped her to stay with the situation, but also to withdraw from it in a positive way. One night she had a nightmare that the client had actually killed herself, and, she said, 'I realised that when I am so worried about her, that's when I get in the way.' Both she and her client had to learn to trust something beyond themselves, and she herself had to come to terms with the fact that she was helpless to prevent the suicide if the client was determined. She therefore turned to prayer: 'When every-thing else feels empty, that's all we have.' Interestingly, she became extremely fond of this client because they had been through so much, and she had learned so much from her. There was a sense of shared helplessness, which forced both to stand back, and into which a third unknown element had entered.

In this particular instance, the counsellor never talked to her client about the fact that she was praying for her and about her, even though she knew the client herself believed in God. A quite different approach was taken by someone whose client had to travel a lot for her work and found these separations difficult. She agreed with the client that at certain times in the week they would both pray or meditate at the same time, and in this way some kind of continuity was maintained. Both the counsellor and the client regarded what they were doing as more than thinking about each other: they were meeting each other in a space which contained a third presence, and both of them regarded this as the basis of the bond between them.

Another counsellor described how she felt she encountered God through her work, although, again, she never talked about this with her clients. Her own parents had both been avowed atheists. She had nevertheless attended a missionary school, where what she experienced seemed to her to kill any kind of creativity. She felt that the pupils were told what to believe, without any regard for where they might be starting from or how they might personally relate to it. In spite of this background, or perhaps because of it, she developed a strong sense that appreciation of beauty leads people to God, and she had come to regard her father, particularly, as a deeply spiritual person in spite of himself: 'He never misses an opportunity to comment on the day, to appreciate the beauty of the garden, to be thankful for a good meal.' To her this was a religious attitude, even though he himself was militantly atheistic.

Her own sense of wonder was carried over into her work as a counsellor. 'I can find God in the beauty of creation by looking out of the window,' she said, but she also discovered it in the mystery and creativity of the people she worked with. 'I think,' she added, 'that a lot of the process is mystical, and I see God in that mysticism. Our creativity is God within us.' To her regret, she had not so far been able to express this in any corporate way, because she had been unable to find a spiritual home in a church (although a meeting with a local deacon, a woman, had begun to give her hope this might be possible). It was when the work seemed particularly hard that she would be inclined to pray. Like many others, she felt that some of the people who came to her needed more than she could offer; and it was in prayer that she placed some kind of trust in something beyond the skills and insights she herself could bring to the situation.

It is often, too, in silence – when to all intents and purposes the session seems to have dried up – that people experience something which some would call prayer. As one counsellor put it: 'You know how in a session you sometimes feel you ought to say something intelligent and connecting and holding and all the rest, and the words just aren't there; but I think that sometimes in the silence that's where the prayer is. And that is enough.'

Twice I have spent an entire session in silence. After one of these, the client came back and said it was the best session we had ever had. We had been working together for some years, so it was an object lesson in non-intervention. The other (with a different person) happened as she was struggling to tell a painful and difficult story which had been locked inside her for many years. Later she said that during the silent session she had felt very held by me, but that the quality of my listening deteriorated once she started to tell the story. She was absolutely right. While I knew only that something extremely painful was involved, but nothing of the content, I was able to be with her in her feelings. Once there was a narrative, which took several sessions to unfold, I became caught up in wanting to know what eventually happened, and my patience was stretched way beyond its natural limits.

What many people would say is that what we find in shared silence is more than a relationship between two people. It begins to access something which belongs to all of us, and it is there that we are in touch with what can ultimately heal us.

A common humanity: modern resonances in ancient tradition

> I will utter dark sayings from of old,
> things that we have heard and known,
>   that our fathers have told us.
> We will not hide them from their children,
> but tell to the coming generation . . .
>   (Psalm 78:2b-4)

Some years ago, the writer Alan Bennett was appointed as a trustee of the National Gallery, and was taken on a tour by the Director (he suspected this made the Director rather nervous about his qualifications to be a trustee of a major art gallery). At one point in the tour he found himself totally involved with a picture. They had paused in front of 'The Baptism of Christ' by Piero della Francesa, a fifteenth-century artist. This painting shows Jesus being baptised in the river Jordan, while other people, eager to join John the Baptist and learn from him, are awaiting their turn. One of these is a man who is pulling his shirt off over his head before stepping into the river. Bennett was enchanted by this man. Here was someone from five hundred years ago who pulled his shirt over his head in exactly the same way that men do today. In a newspaper article he compared this experience to reading a novel. One of the pleasures of reading, he said, is that you can think you are the only person in the world who can possibly have the thoughts and feelings that you do, until you discover, in novels, that someone else has them too. That, said Bennett, is like someone reaching out and taking your hand.

This is often the experience of people studying ancient philosophical and spiritual writings. Although there are some respects in which human life changes unrecognisably over time and across cultures, there are others in which we go on fighting the same battles in our lives and personal relationships. 'The Bible,' said a counselling student, 'contains psychology way ahead of its time.' Perhaps this could be reframed more realistically. Ever since the dawn of consciousness there have been people – poets, artists, philosophers and mystics – who have had a grasp of what we would now call psychology. Freud himself saw his task as putting into a scientific framework what was already known through literature and the arts. In that sense he was saying nothing new; what was new was his way of saying it, approaching it as a science. So, if we search any spiritual tradition we will find there, too, innumerable insights into the workings of the human psyche, even if the terms in which they are described are sometimes hard to decipher, because our understanding of the nature of the world and our place in it may be very different.

The following examples, again, come from the so-called 'patristic' writers of the early Christian centuries, most of whom were engaged in some sort of monastic life. Living among very few people, and with very little distraction or entertainment, they not only had to get to know themselves, but also how to relate to each other. Many of them became extremely familiar with what they would have referred to as passions or vices: anger, sexual compulsion, greed, envy, pride, despair (in the sense of losing the capacity to care about anything). All these are the very stuff with which counsellors work, although most counsellors would not use the language of temptation or passion in talking about them.

In trying to understand what these early writers have to say, we have to remember that their approach is far less individualistic than anything we encounter today. So, when they refer to vice, or temptation, they are really concerned with the state of the world rather than with an individual person. That is, the world being in a state of separation from God, and distorted from the original state in which it was created, everyone is subject to the same difficulties. This does not free us from responsibility for our thoughts or actions: on the contrary. The task of the human being, as they saw it, was to grapple with these things in prayer, to become free of them. The less room there is for, say, resentment against a person who has offended us, or thoughts of the things we would like to possess, the more room there is for God. For them, as for mystics throughout many centuries and many different traditions, the human being is a microcosm of the universe. (Compare, for example, the Sufi saying: 'The human being is the marriage song of the world'.) Any healing – or its reverse – in the individual has implications for the whole of creation. This is something of what a counsellor meant who said, about the effect her clients' problems had on her: 'The better I can get it flowing in me, the better it flows out there.' It is not surprising, therefore, that among these writers and others, we find much astute psychology.

John Cassian, for example, who lived in the fifth century, describes the temptation (as he would have seen it) of dejection in terms which will be familiar to anyone who has suffered from depression. It is, he says, like a moth devouring clothing, or like woodworm devouring wood. In the same way, it devours the soul, persuading its victim to 'shun every helpful encounter and stops him accepting advice from his true friends . . . Seizing the entire soul, it fills it with bitterness and listlessness. Then it suggests to the soul that we should go away from other people since they are the cause of its agitation.'[8] He suggests a useful strategy: we set against each other those things which are attacking us. So, for example, when we are assailed by dejection or listlessness, we encourage anger to fight against it. We can then, as it were, leave them to fight it out, and get on with our own prayer.

It is, of course, a commonplace of modern psychology that buried anger lies beneath the deadening effects of depression. We experience an overwhelming exhaustion because so much unconscious energy is going into keeping at bay feelings which we cannot manage. Nowadays, we see depression in terms of personal propensities – genetic and environmental – and of ways in which the individual psyche has responded to events in our lives, again preventing us from being free to be ourselves. For us, as for John Cassian, the result is that we are unable to live our lives as we would wish, even though the terms of reference are rather different. For him, what matters is that the soul should become free in its relationship to God, and both the despair and the anger result from the forces of evil doing their best to prevent this by their attacks. Nevertheless, there is a meeting point in the understanding of the relationship between anger and depression which provides common ground.

Moreover, Cassian sees the propensity for anger as something that is inbuilt in us, put there, as it were, by God, for our use. It is not simply negative, but a resource which we can use against temptation (though we are more inclined to use it against other people). This has interesting connections with the work of the so-called 'object relations' theorists, and in particular Winnicott, on aggression.[9] They came to the conclusion that the capacity for aggression was not simply negative, but a useful aspect of our instinctual nature: one which we can use creatively if we can harness it.

Again, although it may be couched in different terms, the project of becoming truly who one is, is central both to the counsellor and the spiritual guide, and for both the key to this is stripping away neurotic self-dislike and learning to live with the fact that we are loved. A seventh-century bishop, Isaac of Nineveh, often faced opposition because he refused to engage in conflict. Relationships break down, he maintained, because a false zeal for truth makes us judge others. This is rooted in two things: believing one is better than other people, and believing that to hate sinners is to be God's friend, when it was for the sake of sinners that the Son of God died. (Compare: 'Those who are well have no need of a physician, but those who are sick; I came not to call the righteous, but sinners', Mark 2:17). Nothing, he said, upsets God so much as someone who judges others, 'wandering about among other people's deeds'. He goes so far as to suggest that Scripture itself is misleading, since it suggests that God acts out of anger or jealousy, but these are merely human interpretations. In modern terms we might call this projection: a process whereby we can only perceive in others what we cannot perceive in ourselves. It is often argued that we 'make God in our image', that is, we project onto God the qualities which are hidden within us, whether love and goodness, or punitive anger, etc. The point of prayer, as he understood it, was to discover the love of God, since the more we can get ourselves in line with God's perspective, the more we will value others for their potential, rather than judge them for their deeds.

Another seventh-century writer, Maximos, sees us (in line with person-centred psychology) as essentially good. For him, unlike the modern psychologist, it is not so much our in-dividual story that gets in the way of realising this goodness, as the fact that we are born into a world which has fallen away from God, and which is therefore distorted and distorts us. All our difficulties – selfishness, pride, anger and so on – are deviations from our natural selves, which divert our ener-gies from their true path. Nevertheless, individual experience counts: 'Disgrace, injury, slander . . . beatings, blows and so on – these are the things which dissolve love, whether they happen to oneself or to any of one's relatives or friends.'[10] Such treatment, then, undermines our capacity for love, which is our true calling. Again, the emphasis is different. For

Maximos, such experiences are overcome through prayer, above all in a sincere and determined effort to see everything, including hardship, as allowed by God in God's love for us. Where our capacity for love has been damaged by ill treatment, it is up to us to recognise the ways in which our love is damaged, and not to 'lose our love' in whatever circumstances. Only in this way will we be healed, that is, recover the natural state, in the image of God, in which we were created.

For a present-day counsellor, on the other hand, the path to healing would be more likely to be seen in a relationship which offers 'unconditional positive regard'. This is a phrase used by Carl Rogers, the founding father of person-centred counselling, to describe the ongoing non-judgemental and accepting attitude of counsellors towards their clients. Damage cramps our ability to live, because we become tied in to our anger, and because of guilt about that anger. We are also inclined to believe such damage expresses the truth about ourselves: that we are worthless. This recedes in discovering a relationship secure enough to allow us to express our anger, and which tells us we are intrinsically worthwhile.

On close inspection, however, perhaps the gap closes a little. For Maximos, the heart of the matter is that in God's eyes we are loved to an extent that is beyond the understanding of any one of us. Holding on to that love means practising it, always stretching our capacity for it beyond the point that we have reached, and expressing it in our relationships with others. He did not speak glibly. As an old man, in his eighties, he was cruelly tortured and exiled for his insistence that Christ's struggle in Gethsemane was a true, human struggle, which he could, as a human being like us, have refused (twenty years after his death, this teaching was accepted and Maximos – now usually known as Maximos the Confessor – was honoured as a Father of the Church). In his life, therefore, as well as in his teaching, he demonstrated not only the importance of holding on to love, but also the determination to do it. This is a struggle which we have also seen demonstrated in the lives of counsellors, as they refuse to abandon their clients, insisting by their actions that their lives count, even when this involves a fierce inner struggle.

The essence of the connection was summed up by a counsellor describing how her faith in God (a faith which, incidentally, had little to do with dogma) informed her practice: 'I must say that when I look at the Bible and other holy books, I think they are wonderful psychology manuals. I feel that vision – about working together and walking alongside and carrying each other – has all kinds of implications for dependency and power. Only God has the power to actually carry you. The rest is, we help, lean on each other. Sometimes walking, sometimes climbing; sometimes I see it as swimming. There's always a togetherness.'

5

Minding the gap:
differences in approach

As we have seen, counsellors and clients talk with great conviction and warmth about the positive role prayer plays in
their work together, but this is not the whole story. Other
strong emotions may come into play. For example, in a series
of formal interviews about prayer, counsellors were asked
how they felt about the interview itself. Their answers show
that it was far from easy: 'I was very nervous . . .', 'I was
dreading it . . .', 'I had a great fear . . .', 'I almost felt I shouldn't
have told you . . .', 'I was close to tears.' It was a relief to some
to discover they had far more to say than they had thought;
for others, to be able to share things they had struggled with
alone. Nevertheless, they said, it touched on something both
very divided and extremely private. For these people the
questions were not just intellectual: a way of life was involved.

What is the cause of so much conflict? It is one which people
experience both within themselves and with the institutions
to which they belong. Many who have tried to reconcile
religious faith with counselling practice have tales to tell of
isolation or rejection. Their situation can be like that of the
gay man who said, 'There is only one thing more lonely
than being gay in a Christian community, and that is being a
Christian in a gay community.' The experience of a student
on a counselling course who was told to 'cut the religious
crap' is not unusual. 'I've missed the opportunity to talk about
this during my training,' said another. 'It's very quickly
avoided.' At the same time, there are many counsellors who

have been forbidden to practise their skills within a church setting, being told that counselling is 'of the devil' or similar. Teaching counselling in theological colleges I have often found my approach criticised on the basis that it is self-indulgent, or 'navel-gazing'. 'What's the point of wallowing in feelings?'

Yet those on each side of this divide have a great hunger for what the other side has to offer. On one occasion when I had been asked to give a presentation on the spiritual dimension to the first year of a counselling course, one of the tutors left an answerphone message expressing concern that I might be 'too Christian' in my approach and asking for reassurance. Before I had found an opportunity to reply, another tutor phoned to say that the second years were so interested in the subject that she would like me to stay long enough to do the presentation twice. Similarly, in theological settings, many students are acutely aware of the importance of being able to listen to and understand ways in which people talk about their lives; the difficulty is how to become good pastors, not second-rate counsellors.

Many people want to enter into dialogue, but are anxious that this may result in something too reductive: 'In a way I regret there's been no discussion on the course,' said a student counsellor, 'but in another way I don't, because I don't want it tied down and defined.' This is a serious difficulty whether we approach the questions from a theological or a psychological standpoint. We are trying to say something about human beings in relation to God, and about questions of life and death, and in general we will learn far more by a commitment to unravelling our assumptions in the light of experience – by treating whatever we have to say as 'work in progress' – than by trying to put forward a fixed position.

There is no doubt that the terrain which lies between these two worlds – the psychological and the religious – is extremely thorny, and difficult to inhabit. It is in itself a form of desert. Counsellors face accusations that their profession sells out to individualism, takes a reductive, rationalist view of human life, and produces no solutions. At the same time, members of Christian churches which for centuries have failed to live like Christ, must be willing to hear how people have been damaged within those churches, and open to criticisms of religious practice which can ring all too true. Fr Alexander Schmemann, who spent many years teaching in theological schools in New York, noted in his journal:

> I see that one can love religion like anything else in life: sports, science, stamp collecting; one can love it for its own sake without relation to God or the world or life. Religion fascinates; it is entertaining . . . That kind of religion is not necessarily faith. People expect and thirst after faith – and we offer them religion – a contradiction that can be quite deep and awesome.[1]

This is a challenge which faces anyone involved in trying to live by what they believe, whether their focus is psychological or spiritual. Anyone trying to integrate the two requires courage to hear the pain behind the suspicion and rejection on both sides. To do this while maintaining professional and spiritual integrity can be very hard indeed.

A typical account of the loneliness of this particular journey came from a student counsellor. He could find nowhere in his training institution where it was acceptable to talk about his spirituality. He had hoped that his church would provide some sort of 'corporate pool' where these conversations could be had, but found that here, too, any kind of questioning was unacceptable. Consequently, his experience of training was an uncomfortable and isolated one. Similarly, church members often comment that although they may have spent years in church groups of one kind or another for support and fellowship, life events which affect every one of us such as illness and bereavement, let alone sexuality, are never really shared. In an all too familiar story a married couple described how they had never forgotten being in one such group when their child was seriously ill, and being told, 'You'll be laughing about this in twenty years.' The American writer Annie Dillard has compared church to a cruise ship. Everyone is having a good time on deck, smiling and waving and playing games, while ignoring the deep and threatening swell of the waters below.

This is not, of course, how the Gospels encourage people to live. Neither does it belong with a disciplined and realistic approach to counselling psychology. It is a mistake to assume that either can provide neat solutions. Problems arise when we try to tie down our existence and that of other people to a formula, to cling to answers and make the situations fit, rather than vice versa.

Inhabiting too narrow a space: 'sick paradigm syndrome'

One way of looking at what is going on is to think of the two disciplines – counselling, and the religious path whose practice is prayer – as operating within particular paradigms, or patterns of ideas. A paradigm is a universal exemplar alongside which an individual instance can be tested to see if it conforms. We can look, for example, at an encounter between two people and ask, 'Is this counselling?' (or is it perhaps a meeting of friends, an advice session, or something else again). Likewise, those who practise prayer will have more or less defined parameters by which they would judge whether something is prayer, as opposed to thinking, meditation, having a sing-song, day dreaming, etc. (though any of these things can, of course, be done prayerfully). Making these judgements will be based on certain beliefs about the nature of counselling, and the nature of prayer, and these in turn will depend on particular ways of understanding the world, what human beings are, the purpose of existence and so on.

Anyone who is trying to reconcile religious practice and counselling will sometimes find themselves pulled between the paradigms which inform these two disciplines but which do not always conform to each other. Sometimes they may be in direct opposition. This is a creative – if often painful – conflict, since to inhabit a particular paradigm too intensely can narrow our perceptions and distort our ways of dealing with the world. In modern offices, there is a phenomenon known as 'sick building syndrome', whereby the ways in which office blocks are built, lit, heated and ventilated actually combine to make people ill. We can perhaps also think in terms of 'sick paradigm syndrome' whereby we build frameworks out of our values and beliefs which, if we lock ourselves into them too tightly, are likewise damaging to our emotional and spiritual health.

The counselling world, for example, bases its practice on certain conditions and techniques which are designed to foster trust, openness and growth. These include confidentiality, consistency of time and place, and encouraging people to understand and take responsibility for their own reactions. Their maintenance requires discipline on the part of both counsellor and client, but problems can occur when we forget that they belong to a particular task, and are not necessarily appropriate in everyday life. Many is the counsellor who has been told by family or friends, 'Don't try to therap me!' or 'You've got your counsellor's face on', when offering sympathy or support, or simply showing an interest. The particular awareness of time which is necessary to the work can become a disadvantage outside the consulting room: finding oneself becoming restive after spending fifty minutes with a friend perhaps, or assuming that if someone wants to talk over a problem it will take an hour rather than ten minutes. Recently, I made an arrangement to have a chat with a friend who is also a counsellor. Since he lives at a distance, and there was no opportunity to meet, we agreed a time when he would phone me up. At the end of our talk, I was startled to see that the display on the phone showed we had chatted for exactly forty-nine minutes and fifty seconds. Some habits die hard.

I have also found myself carrying confidentiality to unreasonable limits. At a church conference, I noticed two friends arranging to go for a walk after lunch. One of them is a counsellor. When someone asked the whereabouts of the other friend that afternoon, I immediately found myself telling a barefaced lie. 'No, I haven't seen her,' I said. I had made an automatic assumption that if she was with a counsellor – even an off-duty one – this was a private matter.

More seriously, ways of reacting to people which are perfectly appropriate when there is a particular task in hand between counsellor and client, can become part of everyday discourse in ways that are destructive to ordinary friendship or working relationships. For example, the technique of answering a question with a question is one that is well known and useful for getting to the meaning behind the question. After a meeting in which a committee member had made a number of loud remarks which I found offensive, I asked a friend who had spoken highly of him what it was she liked about him. Being a counsellor, she immediately parried: 'What is it you *don't* like about him?' The discussion turned to my own shortcomings, and it took a conversation with someone else to discover what lay behind his manner and that he had a particular slant on the project in hand which was actually very close to my own.

Again, stories abound of counsellors becoming so locked into the idea of clients learning to take responsibility for themselves, that they behave in ways that can seem absurd or inhuman to any ordinary person. A client phoned her counsellor to say she would not be able to make her appointment because she was snowed in. There was no way she could get the car out of the drive. 'You must take responsibility for that,' she was told. Afterwards, the client was outraged. 'How am I supposed to take responsibility for a snowstorm?' she asked. 'I *had* done the responsible thing by phoning her.' Another client had to go into hospital for six weeks for surgery. He felt he had learned nothing about the value of money by being charged at the full rate for twice weekly sessions throughout that time. 'Yes, I did go back afterwards,' he said years later, 'but sometimes I wonder why.'

In religious circles, sick paradigm syndrome can take the form of an assumption that because we all believe in God, we don't have any real disagreements, and that problems can be glossed over. One must be relentlessly cheerful. A few years ago I attended a meeting of pastoral care tutors at which all the others present were clergy. We had a brief visit from a young woman I shall call Sarah, in whose room we were meeting. The room was available for us because she was ill with cancer, and unable to work. As she was leaving, one of the clergy said to another, 'How is Sarah's health?' Sarah turned at the door, and said, 'I'll tell you myself.' She went on to say that she had secondaries, and was receiving palliative care. There was a momentary silence before one person said: 'You are not really suffering then?' Another added: 'You might have a remission.' Sarah left the room in tears. A year later she was dead.

Religious practice, in itself intended to foster spiritual growth, can all too often seem to do the opposite. There are, of course, countless people who for religious reasons practise all kinds of self-discipline: fidelity in family or marital relationships, celibacy, simplicity of life and so on. Those who do so successfully, do it with an awareness of the power of the temptation to do otherwise, what in Jungian terms would be called the 'shadow': those parts of ourselves which are in darkness, and may contain great potential for good as well as evil. An important point, according to Jung, is that the greater the growth of consciousness, the greater the shadow. It is not finite, but expands as our consciousness expands. Victory over temptation does not come cheap, and saints are not easy to live with. If we ignore the difficulty involved we can find ourselves in deep trouble. Hence the stories which hit the headlines of those who have aimed too high with insufficient support, and fallen foul of abuse, violence or addiction.

Sick paradigm syndrome can also strike at the religious life in the form of an overwhelming sense of sin which paralyses rather than liberates the soul. One of its most common manifestations among Christians is to become locked into the story of crucifixion and death, without any real awareness of resurrection. These two are inextricably bound together; one is never relevant without the other. Yet it is natural for most of us to forget this, and to be drawn towards one at the expense of the other. Many people remain stuck at Good Friday, making religion a matter of guilt, sin and self-hatred.

It is to these attitudes that counselling psychology presents a challenge. The greater our capacity to deny problems, it would say, the greater the likelihood of causing harm; and the more likely it is that we will stay trapped in damaging situations without making any attempt to change. Nevertheless, anxieties experienced by some clients with religious faith who enter into the process of counselling are valid and genuine. They know that they are opening themselves to a powerful process in which people often become dependent, find their relationships changed, and may lose their religious beliefs. Aware that counselling often puts people in touch with buried anger or pain they may be afraid of the effect this may have on family or partners: 'I don't want to become the sort of person who blames other people for all their problems' is the kind of statement made out of genuine concern for spiritual integrity as a person gifted by God with free will. There can also be a sense of failure at not being able to make enough of the relationship with God, at needing some kind of human intervention. If prayer is not enough, one might ask, does it mean that it is my prayer life which needs attention? This is a good question but, unfortunately, it is also one with which it is often difficult to find help.

If, however, we can tease out aspects of the paradigms which inform counselling and religious practice, and ways in which they contrast with each other, it may be that one can complement the other, when 'sick paradigm syndrome' is setting in. We will explore these contrasts and mutual enrichments in three areas: affirming and relinquishing self; the 'I' and the 'we' (that is, the individual and the community); well-being and the path of suffering.

Affirming and relinquishing self

Broadly it could be said that in counselling we are trying to build up ego and in prayer we are trying to let it go, that is, to become open to what God is trying to say as being more important than what we are trying to achieve. By 'ego' in this context I refer to that part of us which is able to say 'I' with conviction: that which is aware of needs and desires and can take action to satisfy them. It is a pity that most translations of Freud (though this is beginning to change) use the Latin word 'ego', when in the original German 'das Ich' has much more immediacy. In classical psychoanalytic terms, it is the ego, the 'I', which negotiates between our deeper, unconscious selves and the outside world. It is more than the mask we present to the world. It provides us with a sense of continuity in our identity, and informs our actions and the way we live. It is, however, far from the totality of who we are, and is affected, positively and negatively, by aspects of ourselves of which we are not aware.

Counselling practice, which encourages self-expression and self-acceptance, is geared to helping the 'I' develop, particularly in areas where past experience has tended to squash or distort it, because without a reasonably strong 'I' we are unable to make genuine choices. For instance, a child who has grown up in a rule-bound atmosphere, where initiative tends to be ignored or punished, learns that his needs and his creativity are unimportant. In later life, he may well find himself tied into relationships where he is endlessly seeking to please others, and, even worse, failing to do so. The failure comes about because he has not developed a strong enough sense of himself to be able to relate openly with those around him. He finds himself in the position of Graham Greene's hero, Scobie, torn between his wife and his lover, who eventually asks himself, 'Do I, in my heart of hearts, love either of them, or is it that this automatic pity goes out to any human need – and makes it worse?'[2]

A person with this kind of background may well make a good start in, say, a marriage. He is self-effacing, and caring, and aware of other people's needs. He works hard to support his family. In the meantime, his capacity for creativity falls into disuse. Sooner or later, as in any family, problems arise.

There is financial strain, illness, conflict with parents and in-laws, or major decisions to be made about parental roles. Suddenly, caring is not enough, because there are too many conflicts of interests. His mother, for example, demands increasing time and attention; his wife resents his absence from the family home, and wonders where the man she married has gone; his workplace wants him to take greater responsibility; his children want him to spend time with them; his church wants him to be parish treasurer. Meanwhile, he has forgotten what it is like to play guitar in a band, or to go hill walking, or pursue the quirky interests which made him fun to be with. Weighing up responsibilities and needs, being able to say no to excessive or impossible demands requires a strong 'I', one which has been nurtured by the very things he has sacrificed, including his closest relationships.

In counselling, such a man might begin to identify the rules and assumptions he took in as a child, and look at how they inform the way he lives now. He may begin to assess these for himself, and decide which ones have validity for him and which do not. At the same time he may revisit both his relationships and his personal interests. What does he feel about those closest to him, and the way they behave? What makes life worthwhile? What is it that attracted him to his wife in the beginning? How does he himself see his responsibilities to family, to work, to his church? What does he see as fair and unfair? What, for him, would constitute a real holiday? All these questions are concerned with building up the 'I', reaching a point where he can move from a position of being driven to respond in a particular way, to being able to choose. The resulting choices may not necessarily be what he would ideally want. He may well end up doing all kinds of things he would prefer not to do, but he will at least know why he is doing them.

Another way in which the 'I' can become distorted is when it becomes too closely identified with the picture of ourselves we present to the world. A young man sought help because he was having trouble in a new job. He was confused and uncomfortable because all the other men in the office called and referred to each other by their surnames, except him. Everyone else was 'Turner', 'Carter' or 'Clarke'. He was plain John. All the others had been to public school. They were not used to first names, but to using surnames, which kept a manageable distance between them. However, when John joined, it was clear he had a different background, and he was made unpleasantly aware of it by the way the rest of the group used his first name. His being different threatened their sense of who they were, which was identified with an impersonal, high-achieving persona; hence he was scapegoated.

The 'persona' refers to the mask we present to the outside world. Certain kinds of school or professional education help to form it; so does our upbringing. It is not a disguise, so much as a kind of filter, and is essential to being able to move in particular circles in ways that are understood by others. We have begun to lose sight of who we are behind it, however, when we find our friends saying: 'Why are you using your schoolmaster's voice', or '... being so intense?' or '... ordering me about like a ward sister?' A vicar's wife decided it was time to take a serious look at her marriage when she received a Christmas card from her husband which read, 'Thank you for all you do. All good wishes ...' and signed with his full name.

In counselling, then, we seek the person behind the persona, or the person who has disappeared beneath the weight of injunctions and values of which she or he may not even be aware and has not personally assessed. As counsellors, we help the person for whom abuse has become a way of life, or who escapes life by one or another form of addiction, or who is terrified of commitment, to identify these patterns for what they are. As clients we make painful journeys into our own reality, and learn to set limits for ourselves and others. All this, of course, has major consequences for those closest to us, who are used to us behaving in particular ways. Adjustments become necessary. This may lead to richer relationships, or may result in their breakdown. It may mean working more creatively, or a complete career change. Whatever area of life is involved, it is likely to take us into a riskier existence.

It is not surprising, then, that counselling does not always have a good reputation in religious circles. It is seen as encouraging selfishness, allowing the 'I' to develop out of all proportion, without due consideration for others. Sometimes it is blamed for bringing disruption to families, or for loss of religious faith. 'Before you went in for this,' people will say, 'you were a much nicer person.' Or, 'Why have you started to question everything?' Those closest to the client may perceive the counsellor as more powerful or more intimate with the client than they are themselves, and sometimes this is true, at least temporarily. 'What do you talk about, that you can't talk about with me?' people may say. 'What's happened to ordinary friendship? Why do you have to pay to talk to a stranger?' The counselling profession itself is often seen as having the biggest 'I' of all, and profiting from other people's distress, particularly in Christian circles. At a conference I sat at dinner with a nun, who asked what I did. 'It's such a pity,' she said, 'that you people charge such high fees for what you do. I have many people who come to me for counselling, and it is all free.'

As counsellors, it is essential to take seriously the accusations brought against the profession. It takes a great deal of experience and self-discipline to honour the process rather than one's own skill. By the nature of what we do, we can easily become vulnerable to the illusion that we are wiser or more caring than anyone else, and that it is our time, rather than the work we do and the received wisdom which informs that work, which is worth paying for.

How does this relate to a religious attitude? At the heart of such an attitude, as has already been said, is gratitude. Prayer is a thanksgiving for the gift of life, for being loved enough to have been brought into and maintained in existence, and offering that life for the purposes which God has given it. A phrase from the Eucharist, 'Thine own, of thine own, we offer thee',[3] expresses the essence of this. Whatever the nature of the prayer, and whatever the circumstances in which someone prays, what they have to offer is already a gift from God.

Part of what goes on in prayer, then, is relinquishing the 'I': acknowledging its origins in the creator, and letting its capacity for action give way to listening. It is the 'I' which is capable of protest, rebellion, control, and it is the 'I' which has to learn to give way in order to allow the image of the divine to be realised. It was because of his insistence that Christ himself had to achieve this that Maximos the Confessor suffered. As a fully human being, it was not a foregone conclusion that Christ would accept death and suffering. As God, his will was identical with that of the Father, but as man he had to make the enormous effort involved in bringing his human will into conformity with the divine. This was not in order to undergo some kind of punishment on behalf of humanity. It was to share totally as man in the consequences of the fall away from God, and by coming through that as God *and* man, to overcome suffering and death. By this he brought humanity, represented in himself, back into its proper relationship with God.

This is a process which goes on time after time in the ordinary human struggle in prayer, and the results will not necessarily be what other people expect. In prayer, too, the man who is beleaguered by his family, his mother, his workplace and his church, may become less biddable. It is not that he has ceased to care about any of them, but he has recognised more closely what he is being called to do, and acts accordingly. If he does this consciously and with integrity, he is actually using the 'I' strength that he has gained in order to relinquish that very 'I' which has been previously disregarded, and which he has had to work hard to reclaim. We can only give away what truly belongs to us, and all too often we give away what we have not yet recognised as our own. Neither prayer nor counselling releases us from our situations, but actually brings new responsibilities – to ourselves and others.

Similarly, it takes a strong 'I' to acknowledge true guilt. 'We must do away with guilt!' declared a priest at a counselling conference, nailing his colours to the psychological mast. It would perhaps be more accurate to say that we need to learn to distinguish between guilt that goes nowhere, and guilt that carries the potential for change. Many people who come into counselling are crippled by a guilt which simply tells them they are worthless. Such guilt may result from an excessively harsh upbringing, or from some form of abuse. Whatever its roots, it is based on a misunderstanding of what it means to love and be loved.

A woman whose brother had been permanently injured – physically and mentally – at birth lived most of her life trying to undo this damage, even though she had not even been born when it occurred. At one level she loved him and wanted him to find whatever happiness was possible, and this was valuable to him. On another level, however, she felt so responsible for what had happened that she was unable to look at his situation realistically, or to accept that anything about his life could be good. Both were deeply religious. He, after years of rage and frustration at the physical and mental limitations of his life, eventually came to live contentedly. He made friends and did simple work. He took church member-ship very seriously, and for him Jesus was a real person whom he loved and who loved him. He came to see his problems as something which identified him with Jesus. 'It's because I love Jesus so much,' he said, 'that these things happen to me.' This identification with Jesus gave meaning to his suffering.

For his sister, however, the grief and frustration never let up, to the extent that when he did achieve something she could take no pleasure in it because it was so far from what he would have achieved if he had not been injured. She herself had suffered as a child, partly because of the strain his dis-abilities placed on the family, and her sense of 'I' was badly damaged. Her life was given over to unrealistic plans to rescue her brother, and she suffered long term from deep depression. He had achieved a kind of freedom, but she remained trapped in the tragedy. Guilt of this kind is stifling to the spirit, and works against any kind of true change.

By contrast, in a less serious but significant incident, a small boy broke his younger brother's leg. It was an accident which happened one afternoon while their mother was out and their father was looking after them. No doubt feeling guilty himself that this should have happened while he was in charge, the father was explosively angry in a way which shocked and frightened his son. The next morning, when everything had quietened down and the leg had been treated, the boy went and found his mother. 'It's no good,' he said, 'I'll have to go, won't I?' Small though he was, this child was able to acknowledge that he had done something terrible, even if it was by accident. As a secure child, he was able to accept the reassurance that he was loved and forgiven. He was able to experience guilt, but also to let go of it.

The 'I' and the 'We': individual and community

Another area of conflict is between the so-called individualism of counselling and a religious commitment to community. Again, the counselling profession is often criticised for being concerned with one person in isolation, though as we have seen, this is not necessarily the experience of those engaged in it. It is true, however, that generally counsellor and client will know each other in only one context, and in isolation from the communities in which they live.

This was brought home to me several years ago by a group of ordinands, to whom I was teaching some basic counselling skills. We were doing a role play about anger, using the situation of a young man who was dying, and who was so angry with his parents that he refused to see them. From a counsellor's standpoint the focus would be on releasing and working with the anger, helping the man to express it and to come to his own decision as to whether to change his position. Such an approach was not only alien but shocking to the ordinands. 'But surely,' they said, 'you couldn't just sit around and talk with him about it. You would offer to contact his parents, and see what you could do to bring about a reconciliation.' They may have been right, but so might I: it depends what you think you are trying to achieve.

The counselling relationship takes place in private, and this is for good reasons. It is informed by the experience and understanding of a great many people, and in this sense is never entirely an individual matter, but its primary focus is the individual. The relationship of prayer, however, even if it takes place in the privacy of one's own room, is never a private concern. Entering into prayer involves being part of a community – not necessarily one which is externally defined, but one which is made up of all those who pray or have prayed. Counselling may well provide a necessary, if temporary, refuge in which to marshal one's resources. Prayer involves turning towards, rather than away from, other people. Any one person's relationship with God is unique, but it is never exclusive; it has consequences for relationships with others.

A situation where one person has been hurt or betrayed by another reveals differences in emphasis. Take, for instance, a woman who finds that after years of apparently happy and stable marriage, her husband is leaving her for someone else. Whether she attempts to deal with this through counselling or prayer or both, the goal is to become free and to be able to move on. In counselling she would have the opportunity to tell her story, to express her grief and her anger, to look at the implications for the future, for herself and her children. She might also come to a greater self-understanding, and discover ways in which the patterns of her own life have contributed to the current situation. Through an honest confrontation of all that had happened, she might find ways of living with the pain, but also of allowing herself to heal and to find hope for the future.

Any or all of these things might also take place in prayer, but she might also find herself confronted by what it means to achieve some form of forgiveness, even after such a betrayal. (It is not, of course, the case that forgiveness is never talked about within counselling. However, many counsellors treat it with suspicion, being afraid that a person might try to forgive without really acknowledging the hurt.) This woman's ex-husband, his new wife and the woman herself are all equally loved by God. How is she to accommodate this if she is also to acknowledge her terrible feelings after what has happened? This is not something that can be done soon, or lightly. To declare forgiveness from a morally superior position is all too often a convenient mask for anger. 'Pray for your enemies,' we are told, but *how* is she to find ways of praying for those who have become, in an all too real sense, her enemies? Her anger may be justified, but how, in the face of such a betrayal, is she to seek out those areas in herself which require healing through repentance?

This is not a question of adding a burden of guilt to the pain that has already been inflicted, but of being able to become open to the love that is offered by God. Sebastian Moore, a Benedictine monk, has suggested that our inability to forgive gets in the way of receiving that love: 'Far from my refusal to remit [the debt or wrong against me] being manifestly outrageous to me in the light of God's forgiveness of me, it is my refusal that is preventing the light from getting through.'[4] That is, it is not a matter of saying, 'I am worse than anyone else, so what has been done to me does not matter.' It is a question of saying, 'Unless I can forgive even the terrible wrongs that have been done to me, and they are terrible, I shall not be truly free of them. And unless I am free of them, they are still part of me and prevent me from perceiving how much I am loved by God.' The implications of these questions are far beyond the scope of this book, except, perhaps, to say that it is a mistake to assume that this can be done quickly or easily, or even completely. They do, however, highlight ways in which the two approaches can differ, even while both are valid in themselves.

The psychological task is to achieve greater insight, to relinquish the role of victim, to feel and work through the anger and grief, and to seek to understand what has happened. All these are important if we are to find a degree of freedom from the past. If they can be managed, they represent an enormous achievement at a human level. They make it possible to avoid bitterness, and to be able to take risks with loving relationships in the future. The religious task is to 'hold on to love' – to go on believing in God's love in spite of everything, even when this means that sometimes we may regard God himself as the betrayer. In psychological terms, it is essentially the struggle of the individual, the 'I', to come to terms with what has happened. In religious terms, while this is still important, the 'we' is involved, even if in practice we leave those who have harmed us to go their own way. Indeed, this may be exactly what is required. A man who had been sexually abused as a child spent many years working through the damage and pain this had caused. When asked how he had approached the injunction to 'pray for his enemies' in relation to the man who had abused him, he replied, 'There came a point when I had to return him to his community, which is the community of saints in relation to God. That is where he belongs, and that is more important than what happened between him and me.'

This brings us back, perhaps, to the fact that the counselling relationship works within certain boundaries, whereas prayer seeks to overcome those boundaries at ever greater depth. Much prayer goes on in solitude, but it also expresses itself in shared worship and particular rituals, which are themselves an important part of the healing process. In counselling there often comes a point where one can say, 'I know what has happened, and I know what I feel', but it is still unmanageable, and something else is needed. At such times people often instinctively create some form of ritual which expresses their deep connection with the 'we'. A woman whose baby had died, for example, and who continued to grieve deeply for him, devised something which she and her partner did on anniversaries of his death. They had no religious affiliation, but they would go together to the grave, with candles, and with sweets which she had made according to her grand-mother's recipe. In this they somehow expressed not only their remembrance of the baby, but also, in the candle flames, the fragility of life, and in the sweets the relationship of motherhood, not only between her and the baby, but through the generations.

Whether it is of our own devising, or something we find in our particular faith tradition, ritual can provide a space in which the 'we' can accommodate what is too much for the 'I'. This is something which is often misunderstood, on both sides. A curate was devastated when he approached his parish priest about another priest who was dying of AIDS. The curate was concerned that this man might need considerable support and help during his dying from someone who knew what was really going on. 'It's not necessary,' replied the parish priest, 'he has made his confession so everything is all right.' It is, of course, possible that the dying man received relief and grace from confession, but it is dangerous to assume that further care was unnecessary at a human level. On the other hand, a counsellor declared: 'Therapy is tougher than confession. In confession you can just pour it all out and then have absolution, but you haven't actually had to stand up and confront yourself and your own motives.' This, too, seems to sell us short. In order to make a confession that involves a real resolve not to go on repeating the same mistakes, it is essential to acknowledge something of our motives. It may not be necessary to understand what lies behind those motives psychologically, although this may be a help in becoming freer in relation to them. Whether we explore these things in counselling or in prayer we still have to confront the same very painful thing: uncomfortable truths about ourselves in the presence of a true acceptance.

Well-being and the path of suffering

> God grant me the serenity to accept what I cannot change, the courage to change what I can, and the wisdom to know the difference.[5]

How do we know what we can change and what we cannot? Any life has its difficulties. When is it right to accept those difficulties and make what we can of them, and when is it

right to do something radical: to leave a partnership, to refuse
to work under certain conditions, to give away our time and
our money or to spend them on ourselves or those closest to
us? These are questions which confront all of us at an everyday
level. If we begin to look beneath the surface of our living –
what we eat, where we live, the economic basis on which we
operate – any one of us will find aspects of this which are at
the expense of or which exploit other people. It can often
seem too difficult to begin to unravel either the history or the
consequences of our situations, and possible changes we
might make.

In counselling we usually make some sort of start on this
at an individual level, but people are unlikely to enter into
this process unless something is already making life
unacceptably uncomfortable. There has been a bereavement,
perhaps, or a major illness, or we find ourselves in the grip
of a depression; we are unbearably lonely, or we are desperate
to be free of a relationship which has turned sour. In general,
counselling refrains from suggesting particular courses of
action. It helps us sift the problem, look at the implications
of changes we might make, acknowledge the depth of our
feelings and relate our present situation to past experiences
and patterns. But it will not tell us what we should do. The
aim is twofold: to alleviate suffering, and to enable informed
personal choice. Counselling is committed to fostering
autonomy, enabling a greater freedom of will and of action.

Nevertheless, there are values implicit in counselling which
underlie the process. Affirmation of the individual goes with
learning to take responsibility for oneself, shedding over-
conformity with other people's values. Reaching this point
can take some curious twists, because our interpretations may
not always match what is going on.

A counsellor worked for a long time with a young man
on developing his ability to assert himself. His shyness made
it difficult for him to present himself at job interviews,
although his qualifications were good on paper. Both counsellor and client thought they had made considerable progress

until the client went for an interview where, faced with a panel of interviewers, he went to pieces. On reflection he realised that he had become good at asserting himself with the counsellor because he knew that was what the counsellor wanted; it was another form of conforming. Their work was not wasted, however: the test in the outside world revealed a problem between them and they were then able to work on it at a deeper level.

Again, I was shocked when a client arrived for a first appointment, and offered to take her shoes off before coming into the house. 'She must have a terribly low view of herself,' I thought, and this informed much of my work with her until I was asked to play the piano for a friend's violin lesson. On arrival at the teacher's house my friend instructed me to remove my shoes: 'He has so many people tramping in and out of his house,' she said. It was a moment of revelation, because my client, too, was a music teacher. Far from demonstrating excessive humility, she was treating me as a fellow professional whose carpets might also suffer from an excess of other people's shoes.

These are relatively minor examples, but they become far more complex when we are working with life decisions: whether to go ahead with a divorce; whether to continue with a pregnancy, when there are arguments in favour of an abortion; whether to give up a successful but unsatisfying career for something badly paid but rewarding. These are just some of the situations where it can be very hard for a counsellor to maintain a non-judgemental stance in the face of decisions which depend on deep beliefs. They may, indeed, be decisions which the counsellor has confronted him or herself and resolved in a particular way, which may be quite different from the client's eventual path.

Because of this, it is important that counsellors, in order to stick to the task in hand, do not set themselves up as moral or spiritual guides. The job is to provide a space in which the client can find out what she or he really thinks and feels, and act accordingly. This approach is rooted in a desire to alleviate suffering; to help the person live more fully according to their own potential.

While this is also true of religious practice, the conflict in world views can go very deep. In the practice of counselling and in the practice of prayer, we may well develop a greater freedom of the will. In psychological terms, this is as far as we need to go. We can find the strength to make changes, and especially changes which free us from cramping conditions which we have fallen into through misunderstanding ourselves and others. Even on this level, however, such decisions are rarely straightforward, largely because they affect many more people than ourselves. A decision may emerge, say, to leave a marriage, even if one fears the pain it will cause to the children, because to stay in a conflictual situation is also damaging and painful for them. Equally, the decision may be to stay, because of certain values, or because having weighed up the effect on oneself and others, this seems to be the lesser of two evils.

A different dimension enters into the situation, however, if the aim of coming to a decision is to discern and conform to God's will. It may be that some people may actually choose the more difficult path because they believe that the truth about their situation lies not in the day-to-day effect on them, but in an overall picture whereby whatever is given lies within God's providence. Even so, the effect of this on making a decision is not a foregone conclusion. A woman who was being attacked by her alcoholic husband consulted two highly respected priests at the same church. One told her she should leave; the other that she should stay. Another woman, early in her fourth pregnancy, was told she might die in childbirth and advised by doctors to have the pregnancy terminated. One priest told her that, whatever the effect on her husband and the children she already had, she must place the matter in God's hands. Another, while the idea of abortion on any grounds was abhorrent to him, thought that her responsibility to her family meant she was not necessarily free to do this (in fact, she decided to go ahead with the pregnancy, and both mother and child survived).

Such stories can lead us to ask what it is that makes some people so determined to persevere with situations of torment and persecution, when they could be free of them. Not only that, but others who care for them would be relieved of anxiety, and they themselves might live a more obviously productive life. We are not here concerned with people who are locked into a victim role – who cannot choose to take steps to release themselves. We are concerned with people who look at the situation in a clear-sighted way, acknowledge the possibility of freedom, and still, as it were, choose to stay in prison.

At the end of Dostoevsky's *The Brothers Karamazov*, Dmitri is in prison awaiting sentence for the alleged murder of his father. He will almost certainly be sent into exile with hard labour. Plans are made for his escape, which he attempts to refuse. He will make a grand gesture, and suffer, like Christ, in spite of his innocence. It is his deeply religious brother, Alyosha, who puts the opposite case:

> Such a cross is not for you . . . If you had killed father, I would regret that you rejected your cross. But you're innocent, and such a cross is too much for you. You wanted to regenerate another man in yourself through suffering; I say just remember that other man always, all your life, and wherever you escape to – and that is enough for you. That you did not accept that great cross will only serve to make you feel a still greater duty in yourself, and through this . . . you will do more for your regeneration, perhaps than if you went *there* [to the mines].[6]

The man to be regenerated is the true human being, already regenerated in Christ. Alyosha is suggesting that such regeneration is not always achieved by the most obvious choice of suffering, and certainly not by the grand gesture. Indeed, even in the days of persecution of Christians in the early centuries, when martyrdom was regarded as the highest calling, it was nevertheless not considered right actively to seek it. It was not everyone's calling to die in the arena. (A story is told of Origen, a Christian mystic of the early third century. As a child, he tried to follow his father when his father was taken away to be martyred, but his mother hid his clothes so that he could not follow.) When confronted with the choice, however, martyrdom was never to be refused.

The task for the Christian is to discover what his or her own cross is: in what way she or he is being called to martyrdom – to witness. The answer will be different for each person; hence the conflicting answers to requests for advice as to what is the right course to follow. Christian tradition does not favour unnecessary suffering; indeed it is committed to alleviating it wherever possible. But neither is it committed to well-being in the sense in which we might understand this psychologically. Because the world is separated from God it exists in a state of suffering. It is the task of each Christian to live through that suffering not for its own sake, but in a way which can transform it – a way which can bring about the regeneration to which both Dmitri, the black sheep, and Alyosha, the monk, refer.

6

What is a human being?

At the end of a session I commented to a client that her situation was troubling because it did not seem to make sense ontologically. When she came back the next week she said, 'I looked up that word you used, and yes, I agree.' We had spent months skating around a dilemma which involved several other people who were waiting on her for a decision and there was no sign of a resolution. The arguments on both sides were all eminently reasonable, and frequently advanced by concerned friends. Everyone was getting desperate that she should take one course or the other. The indecision was painful not only for her but for all those around her. As her counsellor I was feeling useless and stuck.

The word 'ontological' expressed my sense that we were approaching the problem in the wrong way. The situation she was in was full of people being patient and reasonable, but it somehow did not seem to take into account the way relationships operate. Beneath the calm discussions and civilised behaviour lay something which was simply insupportable, not from a moral viewpoint, but on the basis of how human beings *are*. Perhaps the inability to resolve it had less to do with the difficulty of making a decision than with the fact that all parties to the situation had good reasons for avoiding looking at what was really going on. The ontological dimension was missing.

Thinking ontologically means grappling with questions about what it is to be human, not just how we tick, but the deep structures of our existence. An example of the difference between psychological and ontological thinking can be seen in that between the Myers Briggs Personality Inventory, and Jung's typology, or theory of personality, from which it is derived. On the basis of his observations of people, Jung identified tendencies within the human psyche which are opposite and complementary. Extraversion and introversion are now familiar terms, but there are also the less well-known psychological functions of thinking as opposed to feeling, and intuition as opposed to sensation. The Myers Briggs inventory has provided a system whereby it is possible to indicate a person's natural preferences in relation to all these pairs of opposites, as well as to a further pair implicit in Jung's work: so called 'judging' and 'perceiving'.

What these words actually mean does not directly concern us here.[1] What is relevant is what happens when using the Myers Briggs with groups. First, there will always be a rational element in the group who dislike the whole idea, and question its validity. The argument goes something like this. 'What is the scientific basis of this?' 'Observation.' 'But that's not science.' 'Why is that not science?' . . . and so on. Later on, when people have completed their questionnaires and the results have been explained, discussions follow about how to interpret them. Where does each person really belong in this scheme, and what are the implications for the way they function as a group? There usually comes a point where questions are hard to answer because I would respond one way as a Myers Briggs user, and another from within Jung's typology. According to the first, there is a logical answer; according to the second, an answer would take time, and getting to know the person concerned in some depth.

The Myers Briggs is an analytical tool and works logically. It is a system with a sound rationale and is helpful in sifting people's preferences and interactions. If one thing is present, then it predicts that another thing will also be present. If preferences are unclear, they can be resolved by looking at the rest of the profile. The typology on which it is based, however, does not predict in the same way. It starts from what is. Jung named the psychological attitudes and functions, and organised them into a system describing how they relate to each other, but he was primarily concerned with what he was able to observe as he came to know people. Experience, not logic, will reveal the relative strengths of these particular tendencies within an individual personality, and the typology is merely a framework through which we are able to understand something about how they are operating at conscious and unconscious levels. The analytical (Myers Briggs style) approach gives us a measure of understanding and control. The other, ontological, approach involves an attitude of expectancy, rooted in looking at the world with respect for its otherness, its objective reality.

It is at the level of ontology, at the level, that is, which informs a person's view of what kind of world they live in, that questions arise not only between the practice of prayer and that of counselling, but also between different perceptions of what the work is, perceptions which may differ sharply within the counselling relationship where counsellor and client have different beliefs.

An example of such a difference between myself and a client emerged through a dream that she had the night before a session. Although it occurred after several months of work, it had the quality of what Jung referred to as an 'initial dream'. This is one which occurs at the very beginning – sometimes even before the first session – and which indicates in microcosm what the whole working out of the therapy will involve. For example, a Jungian analyst was not optimistic about working with someone who reported in the first session, 'I dreamed last night that I went to the dentist and would not open my mouth.'

As far as my client was concerned, this was her second experience of counselling. She had begun work with someone else after the loss of a religious faith which was very important to her. There had been much that had been good and nourishing about this relationship, but it had ended badly and unexpectedly through circumstances outside her control. So, there was a double loss: that of faith in God had been compounded by what was experienced as a cruel betrayal in human terms, so that much of our initial work involved cultivating faith in the counselling process itself as a way forward.

After a few months, at a point when our relationship had started to develop a life of its own, she had the following dream. She and I were together in an attic room and she had given me the materials with which to paint a picture. I was painting a baby which she described as her perfect baby, and she was delighted with it. I replied, 'But it's not really me.'

This dream occurred at a time when we had been doing some painful thinking (as opposed to feeling) about the previous situation, what was and was not possible, why things had happened as they did, and what different people's contribution had been. It took hard work, but gradually the unbearable became thinkable, and a new process was established between us. Then came the dream. When I heard it, I heaved an inward sigh of relief. It said to me that a sea change had taken place, and the process was underway – something had 'taken'. The dreamer, however, was devastated. Time and again over the following months we came back to that dream, what it meant to her, and how she hated it, and how I perceived it as positive. The dream which I 'liked' and she 'hated' became something of a joke between us. It was after all her dream, not mine.

For her, the dream represented a further loss of faith. In the preceding months she had come to trust me and experience our relationship as nurturing and promising new life. As in the dream, she gave me the materials and I was using them to depict her perfect baby. Yet by saying in the dream 'It's not really me', I was, she felt, presenting her with the stark reality that our relationship was an illusion. It had no existence outside the fifty minutes a week during which she was allowed to relate to my professional self. The real me was elsewhere and refusing to have anything to do with her. By saying 'It's not really me', albeit in the dream, I told her that her feelings were not being taken seriously: everything was reduced to the level of the transference. That is, it seemed to her that while the intense feelings she had within our relationship were real – a matter of life and death – to me they were merely something to be worked with. I only accepted them within the space of the session, and not as part of her life – and mine. At a psychological level, this is a perfectly valid interpretation of the dream. It tells us a great deal about how she experienced our relationship.

I reacted positively to the dream because it seemed to me to have another dimension to it. She was suffering – and suffering badly – from loss of the faith which had made life meaningful. The dream seemed to me to suggest she might find some new kind of faith by which to live. My painting the perfect baby with her materials suggested that the damaged baby within was beginning to find healing. It took place in an attic, the place which in dreams often represents the use of our thinking faculty, and this made sense because of the hard thinking we had had to do to reach this point. At the same time, powerful feelings from the past were entering into our work, which for her were totally focused on me and the relationship. To me the dream pointed beyond this, signalling that something within her was aware of a transcendent dimension to which our relationship was a gateway. This in no way invalidated either the importance of the feelings which were being stirred up by our work, or the mutuality of the relationship in real terms: rather it underlined its ontological status. There was access, through the dream, to an understanding of relationship which was not simply to do with a regression to infantile emotion, but to one which contained and transcended that human level. My saying 'It's not really me' in her dream perhaps signalled the germ of awareness in her that there was somewhere beyond our relationship, and mediated by it, which was significant.

Both her interpretation and mine had some validity, and both found themselves played out as time went on. But these differences in interpretation illustrate one way in which a psychological approach and a religious attitude diverge. It is part of the legacy of Freud to be suspicious of religious faith,

our own and other people's, and it is a useful one, especially
for those of us who are inclined to bury our doubts rather
than grapple with them. The basis of this suspicion, however,
is the idea that the unconscious is essentially a rubbish dump.
The mechanism of repression, i.e. the relegation of material to
the unconscious (in simple terms, forgetting), protects us from
unmanageable guilt or trauma. We and those who are
important to us are preserved intact in our conscious life.
The experiences and feelings associated with them remain
inaccessible in the unconscious, although they continue to
influence us in ways of which we are unaware.

The emergence of these forgotten feelings in the transference – that is, in the relationship between counsellor and
client – becomes the key to understanding how we are driven
to behave in certain ways by experiences we have repressed.
This is why so-called 'transference interpretations' are used to
challenge material which is brought to the session. Complaints, anxieties, eulogies about other people, for example,
may be interpreted as statements applicable to the client's
feelings about the counsellor, the assumption being that the
client does not feel brave enough to make these statements
direct. 'You must mean me' is the essence of what is often
said by counsellors to clients who are expressing strong feelings about other people. It is a powerful tool, and very
effective when used with courage and integrity. It can help
us to discover what we ourselves are contributing to our
difficulties, and brings it into the counselling space to be
worked with.

A religious attitude, on the other hand, assumes that the
unconscious is a gateway to the transcendent. Some counsellors would question, then, the extent to which such
interpretations, while they have their uses, may ultimately
limit rather than enhance the inner work of the client. How
is a counsellor to judge whether the true valence of what is
said in the consulting room lies primarily inside or outside,
and discern whether its external significance is perhaps more
important than the implications for the transference?

For example, a client returns after a difficult holiday break bringing with her an image of Christ suffering alongside humanity. She says: 'This has sustained me for the last three weeks. I wish I could believe in it.' There are a number of possible responses to this. It may be met by silence, allowing it to find its own level for the client. If the counsellor suspects it to be a flight into religiosity which is avoiding the pain of separation, or sidestepping negative feelings about her absence, then some form of 'You must mean me' must be risked. It is also, however, a very interesting statement concerning the nature of belief. What is required in order *not* to believe in something which has sustained one for three weeks? It might be helpful to explore that, as well as relating it to the client's investment in the counselling relationship. It is unavoidable that the counsellor's choice of response will be informed not only by training, and by the context and history of this particular relationship, but also by faith and experience: religious, political, social and personal.

It is perhaps particularly important that counsellors who practise a religious faith should be wary of making interpretations with a religious bias. Nevertheless, resources within that faith may help to underpin practice, and this chapter offers a framework in which counselling could be understood according to a Christian understanding of the world. Three strands of theological thinking are involved here. The first concerns the nature of the human person as revealed by the incarnation. The second takes the Trinity as a model for relationship. The third is a way of looking at the plight of human beings in a world which has fallen away from the state intended by its creator.

Incarnation as revelation of humanity

According to Christian belief, human beings are made in the image of God, but this image has become distorted and opaque through the Fall (Genesis 2–3). The world ceased to exist as God had created it and became subject to sin and death. Part of the work of prayer is cultivating a transparency which allows that image of the divine to be seen. As one counsellor described it, 'I try to place myself where something can come through.' Such transparency is a rare quality, of which the supreme example is Christ himself: 'He who has seen me has seen the Father' (John 14:9). He is himself, as a human being, in the image of God. At the same time, by being man as man was intended to be, he is also true revelation of what a human being is. Yet, being born in time, he does not escape the effects of the Fall.

In order to understand the significance of this we have to clarify what we mean by the incarnate God. The God-man known in Jesus and described in the Gospels was not a super-charged human being with special powers. Nor was he a god taking on the mere appearance of a human being in order to make a point. According to the understanding forged in the three hundred or so years following the life of Jesus, he was both God and man, not by a mix in certain proportions, but one hundred per cent one *and* one hundred per cent the other. Being completely man and completely God he entered into the human condition with all its implications for suffering and moved through it to overcome it.

At the same time, he was not therefore two people, but one person who was both fully human and fully divine. It is not perhaps surprising that two thousand years later it is still a struggle, even for those who practise a Christian faith, to hold these ideas together. The development of this understanding was the result of lengthy and often terrible arguments, not only among the Church authorities. Gregory, Bishop of Nyssa, writing in the fourth century, complained that it was imposs-ible even to go to buy a loaf of bread without getting involved in arguments about the person of Christ (it is a little hard to imagine a present-day bishop making such a complaint). It was also something that came about through experience, through hundreds of years of living with the legacy handed on by those who knew Jesus. This was passed on as story and through traditions of worship centred around the Eucharist and the liturgical year, and not by the simple positing of ideas.

Because it takes time, for each individual as well as for the Church itself, to understand what is being said, the God-manhood of Christ is referred to and expounded again and again in the daily worship of the Orthodox Church.

This in itself strikes at the heart of the difficulty addressed in this book. If something can only be understood gradually, over time, by living it, how can it be defended on any rationalist grounds? The counselling profession, of course, faces similar difficulties. It is hard there, too, to proceed without an ontological basis – a sense of how one thinks the world *is*. From the outside, the kind of repetition we find in worship can look like brainwashing. For someone who is trying to deepen their understanding of the faith, however, it is a matter of going on sounding the depths of a revelation which is too complex for the human mind to grasp with any ease. Which of these descriptions is closer to the truth is not something which can be solved by rational argument.

Within the context of the incarnation, Christ, being both God and man, was totally in harmony with the nature of the Godhead, and at the same time a distinct and recognisable human person, showing the perfection of man in the image of God. For Christians engaged in prayer the implication is twofold. First, prayer should contribute to a growing transparency to the image of Christ in each of us, so that we try to reduce the barriers between God and the created world. In an individual person's life, such barriers are often the result of a damaging personal history which makes it difficult to experience oneself as loved or valued, and all too often such damage has occurred in the name of religion. In order to provide an experience of acceptance, then, it may be better that the counsellor's religious belief is not explicit. What matters, as the counsellor in Chapter 4 said, is that a person becomes able to feel love and to use it. What follows from that is between them and God.

At the same time, each person we meet is also an image of Christ, however difficult it may be to see that, so that prayer is not simply a matter of one's own relationship with God, or self-improvement. It also requires us to relate to Christ in others as a truth which will be revealed at the end of time. In the story of the sheep and the goats, in Matthew's Gospel, the reality of what has gone on in human relationships is shown to be a relationship to Christ: ' . . . as you did it to one of the least of these my brethren, you did it to me' (Matthew 25:40).

When, therefore, I go into the consulting room and complain about my boss, it is not simply a question of my avoiding complaining direct to my counsellor, who may with justification say, 'You must mean me', thereby opening up my propensity to be dissatisfied with authority figures. For the Christian, since the human person is made in the image of God, broken relationships between human beings reflect a broken relationship between God and creation. In so far as we are prepared to work for the healing of those relationships we are involved in the task of healing creation itself. Hence the insistence, by all early writers on prayer and the monastic life, that prayer of itself is not enough. It must go with good practice in relationships, and a sense of reality about the world: not an escape, but a deeper participation.

There is a story of a desert monk who withdrew into solitude because he often became angry with members of his community and this interfered with his prayer.[2] One day, after he had been living alone in a cave for some time, he went to fill his water jug. All went well until he put it down on the ground, when it promptly fell over. This happened three times over, and the third time he was so enraged that he seized the jug and broke it. Realising solitude was no escape from himself or from the need for God's help, he returned to his community to continue the struggle with anger among his fellow human beings.

In so far then, as counsellors and clients are working together towards the healing of damaged relationships, in a Christian understanding, they can be said to be contributing to the healing of creation itself.

The Trinity: a model for relationship

At the heart of the Christian understanding of relationship is a second theological strand, God as Trinity: Father, Son and Spirit. This is also something to which most Christians subscribe, but less often think about, because it is very difficult to conceive in one's mind. Again it is an understanding which developed gradually in the life of the Church, just as it may do in that of an individual Christian. After some kind of consensus had been reached about the full divinity and humanity of the Son, questions arose about the nature of the Spirit. Was the Spirit God in the same sense as Father and Son, or a creation, or some kind of emanation? It is worth noting that the most crucial arguments in favour of the divinity of the Spirit were not philosophical ones about the nature of God, but grew out of the practice of the Church. Since the Church prayed to the Spirit as God, then the Spirit was God.

As with the incarnation, a paradox is involved. There is one God, not three. Yet God is also Father, Son and Spirit, three distinct persons in relationship to one another. A vital distinction is drawn between God – the Trinity – who is uncreated, and everything else, which is created. In Orthodox theology the three persons are not seen as a hierarchy, with the Father at the top and then the Son and then the Spirit. Nor is the Spirit seen merely as the bond of love uniting Father and Son. The Spirit is a person in just the same way as the Father and Son are persons. The relationship between them is seen as one of perfect balance, as depicted in the well-known icon of the Trinity by Andrei Rublev. This shows the three angels who visited Abraham and prophesied the birth of Isaac (Genesis 18). From earliest Christian times this visit was thought of as a revelation of God and thus a precursor of the incarnation. In the icon, the three figures are sitting around a table. None of them is dominant, and each is attentive to the others in an attitude of extraordinary peace and harmony; yet there is also a spaciousness about the image into which the observer is drawn.

The attitude between counsellor and client within the space of the session can have something of this quality: a vigilance which is also at peace, so that it is possible to be alert to what is going on without needing to act on it. When counsellors describe sitting with their clients in silence, refraining from any concrete intervention, this can be thought of as participating in a shared reality. There is the experience of being with another who is able simply to let be without attempting to solve anything or abandoning the other. There is also the sense of something shared, which relates to both people, but belongs to neither of them. This could be said to reflect the love of the three persons of the Trinity, distinct, yet sharing in one essence, in perfect harmony of will.

Living in a fallen world

As a third theological strand, there is the plight of human beings living in a so-called fallen world which is full of division and conflict. It is a commonplace of much religious and philosophical thought that the human person stands at the place where matter and spirit meet, so that human consciousness uniquely qualifies us not only for rights and relationships, but also for spiritual struggle.

Maximos the Confessor, drawing on his predecessors in early Greek Christianity and philosophy, placed a particular emphasis on division of being as a consequence of the created world having fallen away from the creator. There is a fundamental division between uncreated being (i.e. God) and created being (everything else). Within the former is unity, but within the latter are further divisions, all of which converge on the human person. Humans, then, belong in paradise but live in the inhabited world; they inhabit the earth but are destined for heaven; they perceive both with the mind and with the physical senses, and in their own being they are divided into male and female. For Maximos, the human being is

> the laboratory in which everything is concentrated, and
> in itself naturally mediates between the extremities of

> each division . . . the human person was introduced last among beings as a kind of natural bond . . . leading into unity in itself those things that are naturally set apart from one another.[3]

Finally, and this is Maximos's boldest claim, through love,

> the human person unites the created nature with the uncreated . . . showing them to be one and the same through the possession of grace, the whole [creation] wholly interpenetrated by God, and become completely what God is, save at the level of being.[4]

The implication is not that the human person becomes or replaces God, because God is unique, but that through the work of love, the image of God is restored: human energies share in and work with those of God, and this is done on behalf of the whole of creation. The model for this work of reconciliation is the God-man, Jesus Christ.

A further distinction made by Maximos is between the *logos* and *tropos* of a thing that exists (including a human being). *Logos* denotes essential being, that is what a thing really is, and *tropos* the mode of being. According to our *logos*, we are human beings destined for the task described above. How we relate to that task is a matter of *tropos* – our place in history and culture, and our particular story within that. According to Maximos, the fall of the world away from God is at the level of *tropos*, not of *logos*. So, God's plan has not ultimately been disrupted, but his respect for the freedom of what he has created means that it has become distorted in its expression. Thus it remains our essential nature to be united with God, but our mode of being (or *tropos*) within a fallen world constantly militates against that. The world we live in presents itself to us in ways that disguise the deeper realities; we live in a state of misconception about our true nature.

In this way the spiritual struggle is in two senses one of reconciliation. On the one hand, things which have fallen into disunity – essentially the creator and the created world – are brought together in the cosmic workshop which is the human being composed of matter and spirit. At the same time, the spiritual life peels away the many layers of misunderstanding which get in the way of our being who we are, or are meant to be. The implication is not that we are essentially spiritual beings who should disregard the body, but that our true selves involve integrity of matter and spirit. All is sacred, because all is created by God. According to Maximos the spiritual struggle is not something unnatural. It is the attempt to restore ourselves to the state for which we were created.

It could be said, then, that for the Christian, as for the counsellor, the task is to move from a state of illusion into one of realism. The true sense of the Greek word 'analysis' is concerned not with categorising or dividing up an object into its constituent parts, but with stripping away layers so that it becomes possible to discover what is at its heart. Counselling skills geared to probing deeper into a problem are often compared with peeling layers off an onion, an analogy which works well until one reaches the centre and finds nothing there!

This analogy is also sometimes applied – mistakenly – to a way of thinking about God developed in Greece in the early centuries of Christianity: so-called 'apophatic' theology, or the way of negation. Much theology (sometimes called 'kataphatic', or the way of affirmation) attempts to make statements about God, what God is like, and so on. Its primary symbol is the divine light, and describes God in terms of symbols, concepts, and the names which can be applied to him, which are found throughout Scripture. However, since any attempt at description will fall short of God, the apophatic way is also important. One learns to describe God in terms of what he is not rather than in terms of what he is. The primary symbol is darkness, in the sense of un-knowing. The two systems are interdependent and complementary: God is celebrated in every name but has no name; he is present everywhere and nowhere; everything can be ascribed to him, yet he is none of these things.[5]

It is sometimes thought that this means that once we have

stripped away all our projections we shall confront, as with the onion, the nothingness which we have previously called God. This is to misunderstand the tradition. Certainly it involves doing away with presuppositions and entering into un-knowing, but this is not in order to discover nothing, but something. A more accurate analogy, for counselling as well, is one first used by Plato,[6] and taken up by the Greek mystical tradition: that of a sculptor with a block of stone, whose work removes every obstacle to reveal the beauty of the image within. Ultimately, not knowing becomes a form of knowing. It could be said, then, that Freud's insistence that we create God in our image – that we project onto him qualities from within ourselves – is largely correct. Nevertheless, if God is the source of all being, there is a sense in which whatever we project onto God originates in and belongs with God also. We discover within ourselves something of what God is, but always fall short of the full picture.

The project of becoming one's true self, which is involved in prayer, is also of course a key goal in psychological healing: in Rogerian terms self-actualisation; for a Jungian, restoration of communication between the 'I' and the deep self; for Freud making the unconscious conscious, and so on. The assumption is that the environment in which a person has grown up has damaged their capacity for authentic living, just as, for Maximos, our natural state is masked by the effects of the Fall. The religious perspective is broader, but by no means invalidates the personal nature of the struggle. We cannot sidestep the obstacles on our own particular path, but the cosmic story is also at stake. Reconciliation in our personal story and relationships has consequences beyond our individual well-being: it involves healing for creation as a whole. What might this mean in practice?

One answer can be found in the writings of Julia de Beausobre, who was imprisoned as a young woman by the Soviets. In her autobiographical account *The Woman Who Could Not Die*, published in 1938, she writes about the difference between relationships of love and those of enmity. Relationships between friends and comrades, she says, are like a harmonious pattern of concentric circles. They exist side by side without obstructing each other. But,

> There are other lives, the hostile lives of "enemies" . . . their course is perpendicular to mine. They touch me, hurt me and are gone. But at the cross-roads, the point of pain, a node is formed, a knot is tied. This will live on until it finds its right solution.[7]

When someone damages another person, the tangle or knot that is formed exists between those two people, but is also an event in the cosmos. The harmony of creation is disturbed.

For de Beausobre this has psychological consequences. She goes on: 'This is why it is so easy to love your enemies . . . they are so close to you. Tied in one knot with you. Together you form one node.'[8] Thus victim and tormentor are linked, whether they choose this or not, until some resolution is found. From this de Beausobre concludes that it is possible to turn suffering into a creative process. By accepting one's involvement in this knot, and by being prepared through personal struggle to undo at least one's own side of it, something is changed which has cosmic significance.

This position was formed in extreme conditions, but it can also be applied to the torment inflicted in everyday intimacy, where the distinction between friend and enemy is not always so clear. Counsellors and clients are involved together in uncovering stories of the many ways in which human beings have been damaged, by other people, by circumstance, by illness. It is often material which has been forgotten, or repressed, for good reason, because to remember it threatens a person's very sense of self, and there is always the risk that the reality uncovered may be more than can be borne. Often, as we have seen, it emerges in the relationship through trans-ference, and this can make both participants very vulnerable. In the framework outlined above, such a struggle is not only meaningful as between two people, but also as part of a contest which in Christian terms has already been won by

Christ's journey through death to resurrection. To participate
in the suffering is to participate in the victory: the healing
involved is not simply about relief and recovery, important
though these are, but also about the possibility of glimpsing
a destiny which goes beyond mere survival.

The task is above all not to give up: to remain, whatever
the suffering, on the side of life. At one stage in her imprison-
ment de Beausobre was taken ill, and walked fifteen miles to
the prison hospital for treatment. A doctor rebuked her, and
told her she should have got a lift on one of the trucks which
went there. 'That you should be forced to do things by a
maniac power is one thing,' he said, 'but that you yourself
should be silly is unpardonable . . . everything but a constant
desperate fight for life is suicide here, slipping down the line
of least resistance.'[9]

Another thing which is uncovered in working through
remembered pain is the extraordinary capacity human beings
have for attachment, and for concern for the other, even in
the most horrific circumstances. As Maximos himself insists,
our natural state is not one of disharmony, but of unity with
the love out of which we are created. Yet, in the work of
counselling we know only too well that where love has been
abused or become distorted, the journey into restoration is
one which can take us through extreme darkness.

This expresses something of the tension to which we have
already referred: that between the crucifixion story of Good
Friday and the resurrection story of Easter. As in Jung's
typology, there are two opposing but complementary tendencies in our responses to them. One is to be very good at
staying with the suffering, meditating on Christ on the cross,
experiencing our own sense of sin and guilt. The other is to
overleap all that to Easter Sunday, being full of joy, release
and triumph, and giving very little attention to the depths of
pain and death. The hymn for Easter in the Orthodox Church
includes a phrase which is repeated at every celebration of
the Eucharist, and which insists on the relationship between
death and resurrection: *'by death* [Christ] trampled down

death'. Good Friday and Easter Sunday mean very little without each other: victory over death comes by going through death, not by bypassing it. To believe that Christ's death was the end of the story, or that in some way it did not really count, is to miss the whole point.

7

Treading a path through the wilderness

We have been looking at two separate areas of practice which sometimes overlap and each of which involves an ongoing process. Each calls us deeper into the inner journey; each has the potential to inform how we live in fundamental ways. If we wish to live within them both, how are we to find a way to honour them both?

First, perhaps we should inspect the territory which lies either side of our path. Some of it has been mapped out already. Here we shall look at two areas we have to negotiate: power and powerlessness; and the law and the prophets.

Power and powerlessness

> People continuously come and ask for advice . . . and some weakness or false shame keeps me from telling each of them, 'I don't have any advice to give you. I have only weak, shaky, but for me, unremitting joy. Do you want it?' No they do not. They want to talk about 'problems' and chat about 'solutions'.[1]

This quotation sums up a major criticism levelled by the world of faith at the world of counselling: we try to solve the insoluble on a human level instead of paying attention to ways in which our experience, however difficult, may be leading us to God. At the same time, we are inclined to wallow in emotion, leading nowhere. There may be some truth in this, but many counsellors would deny, as we have seen, that solutions are high on their list of priorities. What the processing of experience means in spiritual terms is, quite rightly, regarded by most as beyond their competence or remit. At the same time, from a psychological viewpoint it can also seem that religion has little to do with joy. 'You can't be a Christian,' someone said to me once. 'You are too cheerful.' Another casual acquaintance who had been present at a rather penitential service where I was doing some of the reading said, 'How can you, a modern woman, go on about sin like that?' How can we begin to reconcile all these different aspects of pain and healing, sorrow and joy?

We have explored many examples of what it means to hold back, to let be, and how this can often allow a movement towards healing to take place. Yet we cannot pretend that counsellors are, or even should be, only doing that. It is well known that they have significant influence on their clients. Surveys show that most counsellors in training choose the approach that they themselves have received as clients. More generally, it seems clear that clients draw strength from the relationship. Very often when a major decision has been taken, the counselling relationship is an important source of support for the 'I' while it is carried through. Facing situations they have discussed in counselling, clients will often ask themselves, 'What would so-and-so [the counsellor] do now?' 'Can I really go back next week and not have carried through what we talked about?' 'Is it really possible that we discussed that/ I was so angry (etc.), and she is still willing to see me?' Even when counselling is finished strength may well be drawn from the internalised experience of a supportive, accepting relationship.

Even the 'hands-off' approach favoured by many counsellors, then, provides a powerful model. 'If she can sit there and hear that and not be fazed by it, maybe I can too.' In addition counsellors often do intervene in concrete ways. They ask questions which put a different perspective on the situation, lend books, teach people how to work with their dreams, insist on sticking to boundaries, confront certain behaviours;

they also encourage and celebrate good things which happen in the client's life, and so on.

As the counselling relationship develops, there will inevitably be times when powerful interventions are made, and there will also be times when counsellor and client sit out together their shared helplessness. Both are important in the healing process, and both have their shadow side. A person who comes to rely on another always to know the answers and be strong for them will not learn to utilise their own strength. It is essential sometimes for the counsellor to fail to be what the client thinks or requires him or her to be. If the client is never able to perceive that the counsellor is also a human being who is vulnerable and inadequate, his or her 'capacity for concern'[2] will not be brought into play, and the relationship will not develop into one that is genuinely mutual. Similarly, if all that is shared is a sense of helplessness, this can turn into a collusion in which neither can confront what needs to be confronted. Sooner or later, sharing of oneself with another must meet difference, disappointment, even disagreement, if we are to find out who we truly are.

These modes of relating also have their place in prayer. While prayer involves laying aside 'I'-driven consciousness, listening for what is being given, it also includes vigorous protest, pleading, argument with God. We have many models for this not only in the Psalms but also in the life of the prophets. They answer back, and assert themselves. It is not enough, it seems, to listen passively, nor is it right to let the 'I' take over.

We have, according to Christian tradition, a model of how to negotiate our power and our powerlessness, in Christ. We can look at it in terms of how we understand Christ – so-called 'Christology' which seeks to plumb the depths of the mystery of the God-man. In exploring ways in which people think about him, we find two main trends: Christology from above, and Christology from below. The first concentrates more on his divinity, and his power to save; the second on his humanity and identification with us in suffering. At a conference on this subject some years ago, discussions became extremely heated. As they struggled to take on board the idea that Christ was both fully God and fully man, people realised that their perceptions of who he was had huge personal significance. 'If he was just like us,' said one, 'how can he help? He'll just sink into the quagmire with us.' 'But it's no good to me,' said another, 'if he's got some sort of special power which means he doesn't really go through what I go through. I need him right in there with me.' 'Yes, but unless he is able to stand firm while you sink, how can he pull you out?' Long afternoons were spent in this vein.

It is extremely hard to hold together in our minds as one person the God who empties himself, who becomes completely vulnerable to human brutality, even to death, and who, at the same time, even in the extremities of suffering remains able not only to endure but to overcome. In the icons we see him nailed to the cross, bleeding, humiliated and tormented. We see him also harrowing hell, trampling down the gates of hell (often shown in the form of a cross), as he grasps the wrists of Adam and Eve to pull them up towards him. As a man he died; as God, hell could not hold him.

The paradox runs right through the hymnography of the feasts of the Church. For example, in one of the hymns for the Annunciation, the angel Gabriel is amazed at the message he is asked to carry to Mary:

> How shall he whose throne is heaven and whose footstool is the earth be held in the womb of a woman? He upon whom the six-winged seraphim and the many-eyed cherubim cannot gaze has been pleased to be made flesh of this his creature. It is the Word of God that dwells within her.[3]

This act of self-emptying is taken to the extreme in the passion:

> He who clothed himself with light as with a garment stands naked at the judgement and received blows on his cheeks from the hands which he had formed.[4]

His death is a true death, but by being the death of the 'Author of Life' it makes a mockery of death itself:

> Hell cries out groaning: my authority is broken down; I received a mortal as one of the mortals, but against this one I did not prevail. I perish with him and with those I had ruled. From eternity I had held the dead, but he raises up all.[5]

A young theology student told me he had searched through the entire texts used in Orthodox worship trying to find one verse of any hymn which mentioned death without resurrection, or resurrection without death. 'There are none,' he said, 'the two cannot be separated.' He was tremendously excited by his discovery.

Exciting it may be, but to live with both of these in all their potency, to know our helplessness and our strength all at once, is something that is extremely difficult to maintain. We are called upon to do it in prayer, to relinquish our desire for control at the same time as knowing ourselves made in God's image. It is also at the heart of the counselling process: to be able to face the unfaceable without losing heart. In the words of St Silouan, a twentieth-century monk, we have to learn to 'keep our minds in hell and despair not.' Whether or not we have any religious faith, we cannot do this without faith in something. Above all, we cannot do it alone. Alone we can fall into the depths; it is only in relationship that we can avoid drowning. This is a truth expressed in the daily, determined work of counselling, by counsellors and clients: not giving up, not walking away, maintaining a stance which says, like Christ in the face of death: 'I will come through this, experiencing all it can do to me, until finally it loses its power over me.'

The law and the prophets

> 'You shall love the Lord your God with all your heart, and with all your soul and with all your mind. This is the great and first commandment. And a second is like

it, You shall love your neighbour as yourself. On these two commandments depend all the law and the prophets.' (Matthew 22:37-40)

A woman was looking for a counsellor with whom to work. Some years previously she had had counselling which had gone well. New problems had emerged, however, and she wanted to do some more. She said she wanted someone different from her original counsellor: 'It was an incredible liberation,' she said, 'a real experience of a loving relationship in a way that I had never thought could happen. As well as everything we did together we had a real affinity, and it opened up all sorts of horizons for me.' Now, however, she wanted to explore in a different way. 'My first counsellor really allowed me to know her as a person, but this time I don't want that. I don't want to have to know them.' She did find the counsellor she was looking for, and afterwards felt that they achieved together what she had wanted.

It could be said that this woman's first experience of counselling was a prophetic one. It took place in a room which was full of objects and images which spoke to her. The counsellor was a charismatic figure, who drew out of her all kinds of hidden potential. As well as the psychological healing involved, their work together opened up a buried spirituality which became an important aspect of her life. The second counsellor was a quiet, austere man who worked in plain surroundings. His boundaries were completely in place, his interpretations detailed, and sometimes seemingly relentless. He worked with minutiae, sticking closely to his theoretical basis. Throughout the time they worked together, first names were never used. He remained 'Mr' and she remained 'Mrs'. He, like the first counsellor, was experienced and wise. He could be said to represent the law.

The law gives us order, structure, predictability. It is based in tradition, in knowing what is right and wrong. It sets limits, defines, imposes discipline. A measure of all these things is essential to the counselling process. The lives of the prophets show them to be subversive, argumentative, often afraid and resistant to what is being asked of them. Yet their battles with God result in insight, inspiration, outpourings of joy as well as lamentation and anger. These, too, can be the fruits of an encounter in counselling.

It is too crude a distinction to say that some people work in the first way, and others in the second. There will always be elements of both, but usually the emphasis will be in one direction or the other, and this will interact with the personality and needs of the client. The same counsellor whom we have taken to represent the law had another client who left after the first session. 'I couldn't bear it,' she said. 'He was so quiet. How could he possibly help me solve my problems?' A third was struggling with memories of sexual abuse. 'I know I am safe, because his boundaries are absolutely in place,' she said. 'I always push the boundaries, and I know he won't let me. He can look after himself.' At the same time she described a real sense of warmth and support. It was not love in any obvious way, but it was a deep compassion which helped her to come to terms with her memories.

Love was a word used frequently by the clients of the first counsellor, whom I have described as prophetic. She knew exactly where her boundaries lay, but she took many more risks with them. Although she had a particular theoretical framework, she was cautious of applying these too rigorously. Like Jung, the basis of what she did was, 'If it works, it works', and like Winnicott and many others she was not afraid to touch, to hold, to provide refuge for people in extreme distress. Again, the prophetic mode can be daunting for clients. A woman who had a long history of psychiatric admissions and, even when well, lived in great chaos, said, 'I can't cope with a space that is too intimate. I need clinical surroundings so that I know where I am and what I am supposed to be doing.' On the other hand, there are clients who say, 'I can't stand going to see someone who is not going to interact with me, who just sits in a bare room. I need to know who I am dealing with.'

For both these counsellors it could be said that theory and technique were a means to an end, and that end was expressing some form of love. In the mode of the law, the tradition of the work is uppermost. It is rooted in communal experience, in received wisdom. There is something that works and, as in some religious practice, ritual is rigorously observed, procedures are followed. This can of course generate nothing but anxiety. How can I relax when I might do the wrong thing? Suppose I overstay the session and get into trouble? What will happen if I read the wrong prayer at the wrong time? Paradoxically, however, it can also provide a kind of freedom. There are no decisions to be made. The session will come to an end at the right time, and the counsellor will see that it does. The books will tell us what happens next in the service; we just have to follow what they say. We know where the boundaries and limitations are, so we are free to attend to the matter in hand. Whether we are engaged in a counselling session or in a traditional act of worship, we can let go of any need to be proactive. We can allow ourselves to become open to what is going on without worrying about what should happen next. The wisdom of the individual counsellor or priest is in being so rooted in a way of doing things that it happens without anxiety, that the process – whether it be of counselling or prayer – has been allowed to become part of his or her way of being.

In the prophetic mode, freedom is perhaps more easily seen. It is creative; individual inspiration is to the fore. Again this applies to prayer as well as to the counselling process. Yet here, too, the law is at work, although in a less obvious way. Those gifted with a powerful sense of intuition – the prophetic gift – soon learn that it is two-edged. It encourages us to follow our hunches, and gives us a sureness in doing so, which is inexplicable to those who are more rational in their approach. At the same time it can produce insights which are alarming.

A highly intuitive woman woke up one morning when she was intending to go to London. 'I'd better not go,' she said to herself, 'because of that bomb.' She was startled at what she had thought and asked herself, 'What was that about?' Then she switched on the radio, and discovered that there had indeed been a big bomb blast in London early that morning and the city was in chaos. Such experiences are not at all uncommon, and can be disturbing to those who have them. Like the ancient prophets wrestling their capacity for insight into conformity with God's calling, such people need to ground themselves in something which prevents them being sucked into a sense of guilt or responsibility for events which come to them in this way, or becoming prey to dark forebodings which they cannot keep at bay. Again, in the tradition of prayer, we are encouraged not to attempt to cultivate such a gift, or attempt to use it for our own ends. We are in touch with a reality at such moments, and to seek to control that reality is simply foolhardy. To live with it creatively means involving oneself in a discipline – psychological or spiritual – which is rooted in received tradition and invokes the law as a protection.

In everyday terms, it is often the *interaction* between the law and the prophets that makes something effective. For example, it may take months or years of working through in the prophetic mode to come to terms with the necessity to end an abusive relationship. If we stay solely within that mode we are in danger of taking the whole thing on ourselves. We may simply move from the role of victim to one that is merely grandiose and unrealistic. There comes a point where it is necessary to look at the situation in terms of the law. What does the law say about relationships like this? What is a just reason for a separation? Who will protect me from potential violence while I bring it about? These are questions which ground our personal emotions in the community, and where we may discover that we are less alone than we thought.

In what sense, then, can the law and the prophets be said to depend on love? The law tells us how we should behave; the prophets call us into creative freedom. They demand that we do more than blindly follow rules or offer sacrifices. We

are to treat God as a person with whom we have a vital,
dynamic relationship. So deep and complex is that relationship
that we cannot find it by ourselves. We not only need the help
and experience of others, but it is through relationship to
others that we learn more and more of its dimensions. Part of
that relating is concerned with structure: how we order our
existence as a community, how we learn to behave in such a
way that we can live and work within that community.

The boundaries and 'rules' of counselling are designed to
help us discover some of this, to realise that no relationship
is going to provide the all-consuming perfect situation for
which at heart we long. Again, if prayer is to deepen, certain
disciplines are necessary. They may change, but we go deeper
by pursuing a particular practice over time. But within both
practices, there are also the unpredictable moments of risk,
the sudden unexpected insight, times when by losing control
of what is going on we find we have been changed. It is
through these moments that love reaches us. In them we
will discover the true nature of judgement: mercy and truth
meeting together (Psalm 85).

This is rarely a comfortable experience, because it involves
recognition at a deep level; even at a superficial level it can
be very disturbing. I once commented to someone that
although she was frequently telling me how angry she was,
she would continue to smile politely all the time she was
talking. This upset her so much that she thought about it all
week, and spent almost the entire next session explaining why
there was nothing wrong with her smile. This simple comment
on what I perceived about her was too much to bear. How,
then, are we to prepare ourselves for total recognition? In
small ways, the counselling relationship opens us up to being
known. Mercy and truth meet together in an accepting and
honest relationship. This is also the case in prayer and in the
rituals that mediate God's acceptance to us. In both disciplines
we struggle to strip away everything that comes between us
and the truth; only the certainty of love can make that possible.

Paying attention

'Loving an illusion is easy. It's loving the real thing that's difficult.' So commented a priest, musing on the complexities of marriage. In counselling we take what we call love as it were into a laboratory, and put it under a microscope. We uncover at least some of our illusions, and discover ways in which we appropriate others as actors in the drama we would like to make of the world. Likewise in prayer, there is an ongoing attempt to allow God to be other, to withdraw the images we have imposed, to allow ourselves to go on discovering without ever knowing or expecting to know the whole: 'A God who is comprehensible is not God.'[6]

Preparing the way: praxis

In our final visit to early Christian writers, we will explore briefly some accounts of the spiritual journey, and how they might relate to the practice of counselling. In general, these early writers see the journey towards God in prayer as having three main stages. The first is *praxis*, or the practice of an ascetic discipline. By living in the wilderness, by fasting, by providing for themselves through simple work which did not interfere with their prayer (many of them were basket weavers), they began to free themselves of the so-called passions – desires, material wants, fractures in relationships with each other – all of which block the path to God.

For someone who wants to embark on this literally in our own age, it can be difficult to find a form of work that is appropriate and provides the basic necessities. Some become self-sufficient in simple farming, either as individuals or communities. Others might take jobs involving the care of others, such as the elderly, the ill, or the disabled. Turning to basket weaving or book-binding may not be the solution for people in our own age. A photographic artist who is attempting this kind of life has reduced her living to a near total simplicity. She has abandoned domestic machines for washing and so on, and makes minimal use of electricity. However, she intends to have a computer. Since her work involves photography and teaching, she will use this to run a website where she can communicate with young people who are interested in her subject, and display her work. This was the conclusion she reached after wondering how to combine her gifts with the model provided by early monks.

The ascetic emphasis of the early writers is not intended to suggest that material things are bad, or that the body is not important. It was central to their way of thinking that the material world, being created by God, is good, indeed holy. The aim was not to make the body suffer, but to cultivate awareness that all life depends on God and God alone, and to reduce the compulsive nature of the body's demands. The goal to which they constantly refer is healing; restoring ourselves to our true nature. What they have to say about struggles with the so-called passions, which they often describe as diseases of the soul, can sound strange in a modern context because, as we have seen, it is couched in the language of cosmic struggle. The demons, the forces of evil, attack with *logismoi*, or thoughts which distract us from the spiritual path, but there is an assumption in many of these writers that two basic impulses are implanted within us. These are desire (including sexual desire) and the 'incensive power' which includes the propensity for anger. Neither of these is a bad thing in itself. They can be observed from babyhood, and are with us from the beginning.

John Cassian writes:

> I say this not to accuse nature – heaven forbid! but to show that the incensive power and desire, even if implanted in man by the Creator for a good purpose, appear to change through neglect from being natural in the body to something that is unnatural . . . a man who gives someone a knife for some necessary purpose is not to blame if that person uses it to commit murder.[7]

Our task, then, is to get to know these things in ourselves and learn to use them, much as Winnicott suggests we need to learn to ride our instincts rather than be ridden by them.[8] John Cassian goes on disarmingly:

> I can remember how when I lived in the desert I became angry with the rushes because they were either too thick or too thin; or with a piece of wood when I wished to cut it quickly and could not; or with a flint, when I was in a hurry to light a fire and the spark would not come. So all-embracing was my anger that it was aroused even against inanimate objects.[9]

The goal of the monk was to pray continuously: to become so transparent to the energies of God that there was no room for anything else, so that whatever they were doing, prayer was always at work in them. One way in which they tackled the thoughts which distracted them was to ignore them. By concentrating the mind on the name of Jesus in prayer, there would be no room for the 'demons' to intrude. They would become bored with lack of attention, and go away.

Another strategy was to analyse the thoughts, to expose them for what they were. Some of these accounts will be all too familiar to anyone who has tried to concentrate the mind for any length of time, whether on prayer or study or any other kind of mental effort, for example:

> [The demon of listlessness] is a harsh, terrible demon, always attacking the monk . . . at the sixth hour (midday), making him slack and full of fear, inspiring him with hatred for his monastery, his fellow monks, for work of any kind . . . He suggests to the monk that he should go elsewhere and that, if he does not, all his effort and time will be wasted. In addition to all this, he produces in him at around the sixth hour a hunger such as he would not normally have after fasting for three days, or after a long journey or the heaviest labour. Then he makes him think that he will not be able to rid himself of this grievous sickness, except by

sallying forth frequently to visit his brethren, ostensibly
to help them and tend them if they are unwell . . . [his
mind] is filled with nothing but vain distraction.[10]

The task of the monk is to refuse to give in to distraction. It
involves staying put, enduring. Gradually his ability to repel
the demons becomes stronger; and he is more able to empty
his mind of these thoughts and to concentrate on prayer. We
can relate this to the task of counselling in two ways.

Firstly, the counselling relationship often reveals patterns
in our thinking about ourselves and others. The counsellor
observes his or her own reactions in the session and uses them
to reflect back to the client ways in which he or she appears to
be responding. 'It feels as though you are expecting me to be
angry with you,' one might say for instance, especially if this
feeling does not accord with the reality of the situation.
Working with this can take the form of asking what 'voices'
are going on within the client. What are they saying? Whose
voices are they? In this way, reactions of parents and others
which have become part of a person's pattern of thinking
from early childhood – 'You are too clever by half', 'You can't
sing', etc. – can be identified, and tested against his or her
own experience. When these voices click in in situations which
make one feel bad, one is then in a better position to answer
back. In a similar way to that in which the monk allows
himself to become transparent to God's love, so that there is
no room for the *logismoi*, one may be able to allow the acceptance one has experienced – from the counsellor and others –
to drive out these negative thoughts. We should, however, be
careful of making too close an analogy here. Self-acceptance,
which is one of the goals of counselling, is different from
cultivating a transparency which opens oneself to God in
prayer. However, the hard work involved in both has some
common features.

Secondly, counselling requires us to work at tolerating the
buried feelings which are getting in the way of living life
fully. When we begin to seek relief from a depression or a

compulsion of some sort, or relationship difficulties which we cannot understand, we embark on a kind of ascetic path. We can learn to identify and let go of patterns which have become part of ourselves without our realising. By the time we seek counselling help it is usually no longer possible to carry on in quite the same way as usual: already we have at least one foot in the wilderness. Within the container of the relationship we learn to sit out and endure our grief, our pain, our anxiety, not in order to indulge them, but in order to identify them for what they are, and to become more free of them. It is often within the relationship itself that we learn what is going on.

For example, a woman went into counselling some time after she had had a miscarriage, because she did not seem to be able to get over her grief. For the first few sessions she wept uncontrollably. Eventually this subsided and she began to engage with the counsellor at a deep level; the weekly sessions became very important, and she came to dread breaks and holidays. Returning after one break of a few weeks, she found that something appeared to be lost. She had longed to be with her counsellor, but now that she was it seemed deeply unsatisfying. 'What is the point of all this?' she asked. 'It just makes me miserable.' She retreated into herself, and they sat in silence for some while. The silence began to feel to the counsellor as though it was empty, and eventually she spoke. 'I'm here,' she said. 'Where are you?' This simple statement and the question which followed helped the client to understand the extent to which she, unable to bear the pain of separation, had simply absented herself.

Over the ensuing weeks they began to uncover the fact that her mother had had a miscarriage when this woman was a small child. It had continued to cast its shadow; the family had always seemed incomplete, and her mother constantly referred to it, even forty years later. The surviving child felt that she had never been able to fill the void that this loss had left behind. Gradually she realised two things. One was that, although she continued to feel sad about the baby she herself had lost, the acute grieving had subsided; some kind of healing was possible. The second was that her family experience had taught her that grief never heals: it just generates more pain. Alone and with the counsellor she gradually sifted her own reactions to loss and separation. Years later, in another context, she was able to say, 'I've finally realised that you can miss someone, and it's OK. It's painful, but it doesn't mean I've ceased to exist.' By sitting out the pain of her story she was no longer overwhelmed by it; her sense of hopelessness was overcome.

In a similar way the monk who endures the mid-day demon gradually finds that he can repel him more easily. It may still be hot and uncomfortable, and his stomach empty, but he has learned that if he sticks it out, his prayer is deepened. The determination of the grieving woman to confront the depths of her feelings helped her to learn something of the landscape of grief, and that it was not a dead end. There was a new place beyond, from which she was able to tolerate loss and separation in a new way, and even to find value in them.

For counsellors, too, this kind of struggle is necessary. We cannot accompany others to places where we ourselves are not prepared to go. This accords with the principle that prayer, in seeking to heal our relationship with God, goes hand in hand with good practice in relationships. 'Take care,' wrote Evagrios of Pontus, who was John Cassian's teacher, 'that, while appearing to cure someone else, you do not yourself remain uncured, in this way thwarting your prayer.'[11]

Many counsellors have first become interested in the work through being clients themselves, and it is now mandatory on most training courses to spend some time in 'the other chair'. My heart sinks, however, when I get a phone call saying, 'I'm on a course and I've got to do so many sessions with a counsellor', as though this is a regrettable necessity in order to get a diploma. Unless we can see the need for that before we start, our capacity to help others in this particular way is likely to remain limited. The experience of being a client, and ongoing inner work on oneself, is at the heart of what, for counsellors, we could call *praxis.*

There are other aspects which are also important. One is learning to live with the discipline of a weekly rhythm, arranging one's life and family responsibilities in such a way that one is consistently and reliably available. Running a practice, especially from one's own home, has profound implications for social and family life, which everyone has to work out for themselves. A counsellor was recently horrified to find that when his small son approached him while he was writing up his notes, he said, 'Wait until I've finished this.' Afterwards he thought, 'I wouldn't treat one of my clients like that.' Again, holidays become significant not only for oneself but for one's clients. They have to be carefully planned and announced in advance, and every absence has to be worked with both before and afterwards. It is quite common for counsellors to find that a holiday, far from being relaxation, is taken up with a kind of bloodletting. So much emotion has been processed in order to achieve it, that in the sudden absence of the normal routine they can find themselves overwhelmed with exhaustion, or anxiety, or physical illness. It takes time to adjust to being merely oneself, when one is used to being so many things for different people.

There are also the pressures of maintaining confidentiality. When I became a counsellor, having previously worked in a small publishing company, I realised one of the great losses was not to be able to talk and tell stories about work. The answer 'Counselling' to the question 'What do you do?' is not exactly a non-starter, because it sets up all sorts of expectations: 'Are you watching us all the time?', 'Are you analysing what goes on?', but it is not possible to be entertaining about one's work as one can be about, say, a day at the office. More seriously, there is a burden involved in carrying a lot of story for other people, without sharing those stories with others except in supervision. You never know what connections might be made.

Learning to pay attention: physike

The next stage on the journey of prayer is *physike,* or the contemplation of nature. Contemplation in this sense means developing awareness of all creation as a revelation of God, and therefore an object of reverence. This is not pan-theism, which treats everything in nature as god. It is more a kind of pan-en-theism, that is discovering God *in* everything, including other people. 'Blessed is the monk,' wrote Evagrios, 'who regards every man as God after God.' We have already seen that some counsellors discover something of this in the process, and see God in the struggles of their clients to over-come their problems. The attitude of any counsellor towards his or her clients is above all one of respect for another human being. In a framework which regards that human being as an image of Christ, such respect becomes in itself a form of prayer.

Contemplation also increases our tolerance for not knowing. According to Maximos the Confessor, this is vital to developing our understanding: we must constantly look among created things for what we do *not* know. The more we do this, the more we will realise the depths of our ignorance, and this enables us to understand 'many great and wonderful things; for to think that one knows prevents one from advancing in knowledge.'[12] We get to know a person in the same way that we get to know God, by allowing ourselves not to know, by peeling away our assumptions so that we are able to see clearly what is in front of us. If we already know, then there is nothing interesting for us to learn. We may have experience of the landscape through which a client is moving – a bereavement, remembering sexual abuse, mid-life crisis or whatever – but only they can tell us what the particular significance of that landscape is for them. It may be something quite different from what we assume.

Knowing better than the client is only one step away from judgement, something condemned alike in the life of prayer and in counselling practice. 'Christ's death on the cross,' says

Maximos the Confessor, 'is a judgement of judgement'.[13] By being prepared not to judge or condemn, a counsellor is actively sharing with the other in the condition of being human, and imperfect, rather than setting him or herself up as a higher authority. There are many stories from desert monasticism of refusals to judge others. For example, an elder was called to the trial of a monk who had been caught in some serious misdemeanour, but he refused to come. Eventually, when they pressed him, he began the journey, dragging behind him an old basket with a hole in it which he had filled with sand. The other elders asked him what this meant. 'It is my sins running out behind me,' he replied, 'and I do not notice them. That is how I am coming today to judge the sins of another.'[14] The trial was cancelled, and the monk pardoned.

In the counselling setting, a determination not to judge or condemn not only enables clients to accept themselves. It also means actively sharing with them in the condition of being human, rather than setting oneself up as a higher authority.

Towards contemplation of God: theoria

The final, but not finite, stage of the journey, is contemplation of God himself, not only through the revelation of creation, but by direct experience. This does not mean we know everything about God, but that we are united with him. Neither does it mean we have essentially become God, but we have allowed ourselves to become suffused by his energies. It is not something that is ever fully accomplished; to whatever extent we participate in God's energies there will always be further to go. In this way it involves living with an intense longing which is never fully satisfied, but it is not, on the surface, a dramatic phenomenon. It is not demonstrated by extravagant ecstasies. In a strange way it appears as a kind of calm, which at most may give an impression of light or quiet joy within the person. At this level we have gone beyond what can be described in the language we have been using of the counselling relationship.

Perhaps, however, we can draw something from this scheme which is fundamental to our enterprise, to some kind of integration of these two practices: prayer and counselling. For all the friction which exists between them, they share a fundamental attitude of respect for the other, an attitude which in practice must learn to let be, to attend to what is, rather than attempt to shape others to our own assumptions of how they should be. The ascetic struggle of the desert monks was geared to this – to clearing away the rubble so that there was room for God in their hearts. It was a journey of discovery which they never expected to complete. Perhaps, then, we can end our exploration with a commitment to un-knowing. The territory through which we have been passing is one created out of experience, that of people working in the modern world, as well as that of people long dead. If anything emerges, it is that no one of us ever sees the whole story – our own or anyone else's. This is why we can never actually tell someone else where to go from here. We can point out landmarks and possible consequences, but each person's journey towards God is unique. The more we pay attention, the more we will be aware of this – of our differences as well as of our common vocation. We can only speak, each one of us, for ourselves.

Notes

Introduction

1. Maximos the Confessor, Introduction to Four Hundred Texts on Love, *The Philokalia*, tr. Palmer, Sherrard and Ware (Faber and Faber, 1981), vol. 2, p. 52.

1: Prayer and counselling: two kinds of relationship

1. See *Pass It On*: the story of Bill Wilson and Alcoholics Anonymous (AA Publications).
2. See, for example, Orlinsky and Howard (1985), 'Process and Outcome in Psychotherapy' in Bergin and Garfield, *Psychotherapy and Behaviour Change* (Wiley and Sons, 1994).

2: Talking with people who pray

1. Canon for Matins, fourth Sunday in Lent, canticle seven, third troparion, in *The Lenten Triodion*, tr. Mother Mary and Archimandrite Kallistos Ware (Faber and Faber, 1978), pp. 357ff.
2. See Patrick Casement, *On Learning from the Patient* (Routledge, 1985), especially chapter 3. The idea is that supervision is not limited to the actual sessions, but the supervisor becomes part of the counsellor's internal world, and available to him or her for use.
3. D.W. Winnicott, *Home is Where We Start From* (Penguin, 1986), p. 154.

3: Praying for others: pitfalls, dilemmas and quick fixes

1. Penguin, 1992, p. 419.
2. Irina Ratushinskaya, 'Believe Me', in *Pencil Letter* (Bloodaxe Books, 1986).
3. Metropolitan Anthony of Sourozh, 'Living Prayer', in *The Essence of Prayer* (Darton, Longman and Todd, 1986), p. 74.

4: Why Pray? Prayer and the counselling relationship working together

1. Marie-Louise von Franz, 'The Role of the Inferior Function in Psychic Development', *Lectures on Jung's Typology* (Spring Publications, 1971), p. 80.
2. Quaker Tapestry, panel A2.

3. Basil the Great, *Greater Rules*, 7 (PG 31, 933). The initials 'PG' refer to the Greek, as opposed to the Latin, collection of patristic writings (i.e. those of the so-called Fathers of the Church): *Patrologia Cursus Completus*, Series Graeca, J-P Migne (Paris). They are a way of identifying where particular passages may be found in the accepted corpus. For practical purposes, there are many translations available of individual fathers, and a number of anthologies, such as *Drinking from the Hidden Fountain: a patristic breviary*, ed. Thomas Spidlik (New City, 1992), which includes the above quotation. A very helpful commentary on what these writers thought about various aspects of Christian teaching, with extensive original texts, is *The Roots of Christian Mysticism* by Olivier Clément (New City, 1997).

4. Stairway to Paradise 30, PG 88, 1156.

5. The Rev. Beau Stephenson, in a talk (unpublished) given to the Oxford Psychotherapy Society, February 2000.

6. D.W. Winnicott, 'True and False Self' (1960) in *The Maturational Processes and the Facilitating Environment*, Institute of Psycho-Analysis (Karnac Books, 1990).

7. For an in-depth discussion of this from a Jungian perspective, see Mario A. Jacoby, *Longing for Paradise* (Sigo Press, 1985).

8. On Dejection, in John Cassian, *On the Eight Vices*, in *The Philokalia*, vol. 1, tr. Palmer, Sherrard and Ware (Faber and Faber, 1977).

9. D.W. Winnicott, *The Child, the Family and the Outside World* (Penguin, 1964), especially the last chapter.

10. Fourth Century on Love, 81, in *The Philokalia*, tr. Palmer, Sherrard and Ware (Faber and Faber, 1990), vol. 2. (A 'century' is a collection of 100 short texts intended for slow, meditative reading, one at a time.)

5: Minding the gap: differences in approach

1. *The Journals of Father Alexander Schmemann 1973–1983* (St Vladimir's Seminary Press, 2000), p. 52.

2. Graham Greene, *The Heart of the Matter*, Book 3, part 1, i (Vintage, 2001).

3. A phrase from the Orthodox Liturgy, which occurs immediately before the offering of the bread and wine in the Eucharist.

4. Sebastian Moore, *The Crucified Jesus is No Stranger* (Paulist Press, 1977).

5. Alcoholics Anonymous: 'The Serenity Prayer'.

6. Fyodor Dostoevsky, *The Brothers Karamazov*, tr. Pevear and Volkhonsky (Everyman, 1997).

6: What is a human being?

1. There are a number of useful introductions to this scheme. A good starting point is Isabel Briggs Myers and Peter Myers, *Gifts Differing* (Consulting Psychologists Press, 1980).

2. See Graham Gould, *The Desert Fathers on Monastic Community* (Clarendon Press, 1993), p. 161.

3. Ambigua 41, tr. Andrew Louth, in A. Louth, *Maximos the Confessor* (Routledge, 1996).
4. ibid.
5. For this explanation of the distinction between apophatic and kataphatic theology, I am indebted to Bishop Kallistos Ware, and his lectures on the Greek Mystical Theology at the Theology Faculty of Oxford University.
6. Phaedrus, 252-4.
7. Julia de Beausobre, *The Woman Who Could Not Die* (Chatto and Windus, 1938), p. 171.
8. ibid., p. 171.
9. ibid, p. 265.

7: Treading a path through the wilderness

1. *The Journals of Father Alexander Schmemann 1973-1983* (St Vladimir's Seminary Press, 2000), p. 130.
2. A phrase from D.W. Winnicott, who uses it to refer to a process in the development of the 'I', whereby we come to terms with our own destructiveness, and learn to protect those we love from it. See *The Maturational Processes and the Facilitating Environment,* Institute of Psycho-Analysis (Karnac Books, 1990), part one, paper 6.
3. Doxasticon from Great Vespers of the Annunciation in *The Festal Menaion,* tr. Mother Mary and Archimandrite Kallistos Ware (St Tikhon's Seminary Press, 1998), p. 440.
4. Service for the Thursday evening in Holy Week, Antiphon 10.
5. Vespers of Holy Saturday in *The Lenten Triodion,* tr. Mother Mary and Archimandrite Kallistos Ware (Faber and Faber, 1978), p. 656.
6. Attributed to Athanasius, PG 28 597d.
7. On Avarice, in John Cassian, *On the Eight Vices,* in *The Philokalia,* vol. 1, tr. Palmer, Sherrard and Ware (Faber and Faber, 1977), p. 78.
8. D.W. Winnicott, *Home is Where We Start From* (Penguin, 1986).
9. On Avarice, in Cassian, *On the Eight Vices,* pp. 85-6.
10. On Listlessness, in Cassian, *On the Eight Vices,* pp. 88-9.
11. On prayer, 25.
12. Third Century on Love, 81.
13. Questions to Thalassius, 43 (PG 90, 408).
14. Sayings of the Desert Fathers, Moses, 2 (PG 65, 281-3).

Index